Dedicated to my friends, of course.

Introduction

Few would argue against the idea that the group of people you surround yourself with will dictate the course of your life more than any other factor. This is true not just for extroverts, but for introverts as well. Regardless of the amount of time we choose to share with others, that connection has an outsized impact on our lives.

Think back to your most positive memories. How many didn't involve other people? Few or none, most likely. How about the periods of your life where you grew the most as a person? Weren't friends or mentors guiding or supporting you? Even the hardest times in your life were most likely made better because of others.

This book is based on a simple principle, that the people and friendships in our lives are important. They're important enough to think about social skills consciously, and to put effort into improving them. They're important enough to justify doing hard work to make ourselves better friends and family members.

The people you interact with could be slotted into three categories. There are acquaintances, friends, and members of your close friend group. Each of these categories requires you to share a different part of yourself, and brings a critical benefit into your life.

Through reading this book, you should be able to make strangers into acquaintances that like you. You'll learn the art of conversation and how to share the best parts of you in an honest and authentic way. You'll learn how to make new friends, and how to be the kind of friend that people want to have. And, last, you'll learn how to build a group of friends with whom you'll share support, quality time, and love.

If you don't understand why you don't have more friends, or if the process of making them frustrates you, you'll be able to start from scratch and build a completely new social life. If you have good social skills but find certain social situations puzzling, this book should eliminate that confusion. And even if you have great friends and have no problems making new ones, I hope that you'll learn a few things to make those relationships even better. Some friendships you'll have for life, so even a small improvement can be important.

Few people excel at any skill without thoughtful consideration and practice, and social skills are no exception. I went from being an introvert who was too shy to interact with friends-of-friends, to someone with amazing friends all over the world, and a core group of close friends with whom I share much of my life. By understanding the skills and principles that underpin social interaction, whether with strangers or best friends, you can break out of any mold you may find yourself in, and build superhuman social skills.

Social Skills are Skills

If you were bad at, say, badminton, you'd probably do something about it. You wouldn't feel bad about yourself, but you'd take steps to improve. Maybe you'd read books, watch some videos, ask friends for help, or take lessons. No matter which path you took, you'd practice. You would analyze your progress and the results of your practice, and you'd make course corrections.

When you finally got good at badminton, you might share the story of how you improved, and would expect that people would generally look favorably on your course of actions. You identified an area of your life that needed improvement, you came up with steps to turn it into a strength, you executed on that plan, and you succeeded.

Although we use the phrase "social skill", we treat social skills more like a mystic inborn force than an actual practicable skill. We act as if social skills are genetically predetermined, like hair color or eye color. If we have poor social skills, or inconsistent social skills, we generally accept that that's our lot in life.

Maybe this comes from the idea that learning badminton isn't changing oneself, but learning social skills is. The way we interact with others is so core to our experience in life that we equate it to who we are. And there's some truth to that, too. How we portray ourselves to others will define their experience of who we are. The same person is considered a jerk and a saint to two different people, not because he actually is either of those things, but because of how he treats them.

Generally speaking, change is scary, especially for friends of the person who is changing. Insecurities surface, as do questions of motives. Why is he trying to become someone he's not? Why can't he just be himself?

But what is self-improvement if it's not actually transforming us into better versions of ourselves? We keep the good things about ourselves, maybe even make them better, but we also attack our weaknesses and reduce or eliminate them. We all have deficiencies and can be better.

It's about time social skills were treated like skills, and any stigma associated with improving them was left behind. We should encourage people who take the brave step of admitting that something so core to their being needs improvement, even when that person is ourself. Yes, we'll become different people, but we were going to do that anyway. We change all the time, usually in imperceptible increments, so why not guide that change?

A Word on Manipulation

I gave a speech at a university once, followed by a
Q&A. The questions from the students were sharp,
leading to interesting discussion. Near the end a
professor asked, in a rather accusatory way, if
practicing social skills wasn't just manipulating and
lying to people.

Many people think that consciously improving one's
social skills is manipulative, deceptive, or
disingenuous. If you're anything like that professor,
it's unlikely anything I can say will change your
mind. This reaction, as best I can tell, is borne from
insecurity that can't be erased through a few
paragraphs of explanation.

I see learning social skills as the exact opposite. To
me, it's the practice of becoming the very best person
you can be, maximizing what you have to offer
others. It's about communicating who you are as
clearly as possible, and removing barriers preventing
you from understanding others with that same clarity.
It's about really understanding what others are
looking for in a conversation or in a friend, and
working to give them that very thing, if you are so
capable. We do things all the time with the intention
of eliciting a result from someone else. That alone is
not manipulation. I might tell a joke to make a friend
laugh. Technically I have taken an action to
precipitate a reaction from him, but few would call
that manipulative.

Manipulation has a connotation of ulterior motives. It implies that we can get someone to do something against their will or better interests by cajoling them or presenting a false impression of ourselves.

That's not at all the goal of building social skills. The goal is to understand better what other people really want, to identify where that intersects with what you want, and to have the social tools required to get both people what they're hoping for. It's also about understanding where there isn't an intersection, and moving on.

The tools we use to do this are self-awareness, situational awareness, good communication skills, and an understanding of humor, empathy, and social dynamics. Some will dismiss this practice as manipulation, but I think that's a pretty big stretch.

Maybe the litmus test most easily comprehended on an emotional level is this: if a stranger worked hard to be a better conversationalist, would you hold it against him when you had a great conversation with him? If you found out that one of your best friends worked hard to be the best friend they could be, would you be offended, or would you be flattered?

In this book, I will be unabashedly analytical, examining and quantifying aspects of social skills that are usually not spoken about. We'll talk about power dynamics, our value as friends, opportunity cost, and efficient use of time. Whether or not we acknowledge these, and other, factors, they underpin our social interactions and play an enormous role in the quality of relationships in our lives. Some find these topics unpalatable, or even offensive, but it's hard to make a better sausage if you don't take a look at what's going inside the factory.

Goals Of This Book

We have a social problem in our society. Our social time is being siphoned from real life into cyberspace. We may have hundreds of Facebook friends whose every move we follow, but with whom we never have a meaningful conversation. So many of our conversations are electronic that we've dulled some of those skills that are only useful in real life: timing, yielding, listening, and perceiving facial expressions and body language.

Maybe you feel the effects of this degradation. You have tons of friends, but few or none whom you could really rely upon, and fewer who really understand you. When you do spend time with your friends, it's not as satisfying of an experience as you remember from your childhood.

The remedy for this problem, on an individual basis, is to build up certain social skills to a baseline level. Before we get into the how of building these social skills, I'd like to give you an idea of the goals we'll be working towards, and why they are important.

1. Be Comfortable With All Strata of Society

A socially skilled person is able to get along with people across all strata of society. Not necessarily every person, but every type of person. This is a useful skill and it's also a very important benchmark. You could rely on commonality with a clone of yourself, but must truly exercise your social skills when trying to relate to someone with whom you have little in common. If you cannot do that, then you may be skilled at relating to people with whom you are compatible with, but not be socially skilled.

Commonality is a shortcut to rapport, and a good one to use if it's available. But sometimes the most interesting conversations and friendships happen between people with little commonality. After all, by definition, if you have less in common there's more new territory to explore.

Building this skill requires travel outside of one's comfort zone, as well as grappling with hidden insecurity. On one end of the spectrum it's possible to feel inferior to people you admire, as though you don't have any value to add to the relationship. On both ends, lack of commonality can be a hard barrier to cross, especially if it's apparent that you're from different backgrounds and the other person is intimidated by it.

Someone who is comfortable interacting and befriending people in all strata of society will feel comfortable in nearly every situation, confident in his ability to add to any interaction of which he's a part. He'll have more opportunities to share what he knows with others, as well as the ability to learn from experiences that he may never have personally.

2. Be A Net Addition

Beyond just getting along with people in all strata of

society, you want to generally be a net positive to any social situation in which you're placed. If someone was eating alone, and you were to join them, that should make their lunch better. If a few friends are having tea together, and you get invited, your presence should make everyone have a better time. And if you go to a large party or event, even though your impact will be proportionally smaller due to the size, those you interact with should be glad that you were at the party.

Being a net addition is different than just not being a net negative. Being simply neutral is often a negative, as you are taking up an attendance slot that could have been used by someone else who could have been an addition. It's important to proactively add to social situations.

Most social circles are actually series of concentric circles. There's the small inner nucleus of people who organize and get invited to everything, and without whom events wouldn't even happen. Then there's the next ring of people who are always welcome, but would never displace a member of the nucleus. Outside those two circles are people who usually get invited, but only if space permits. Or maybe they have certain personality quirks that make them incompatible with others in that circle, meaning the core group must choose who gets invited and who doesn't.

The nucleus is comprised of the people who are net additions, and who orchestrate events. The next circle is those who are also net additions. The circle further out are people who are "not negative". Sometimes they add, sometimes they're neutral. They're nice to have around, but not a sure enough thing to make sure they come to every event. Beyond those rings are people who are sometimes or always net negatives.

By ensuring that you're always a net addition, even if you're not a huge one, you will dramatically increase the number of events to which you are invited. Besides being fun and valuable, these invitations will provide you with events at which you can practice your social skills, creating a virtuous cycle.

3. Build A Quality Friend Group

With the possible exception of your daily habits, nothing will influence your life so much as your core friend group. Whether you're aware of it or not, you are constantly molded and influenced by those closest to you. You'll receive advice from them, absorb their mannerisms and habits, and even subconsciously adopt some of their opinions.

Most people's friend groups are the product of happenstance and momentum. With so much on the line, choosing those closest to you should be a very deliberate decision. The opportunity and ability to methodically build a social circle will improve your life as well as the lives of those in the circle.

The goal is to build a social circle that will both challenge and support you, depending on what you need at the time. The right friend group will be a case of the sum being greater than the parts, all friends advancing more easily through life, enjoying the ride more, and learning more.

4. Establish Emotional Independence From Acquaintances and Strangers

We all need emotional support from time to time. Whether it's someone to sit down and empathize with you during a tough time or someone to cheer you up when you're in a bad mood. However, it's important to get that support from the right people, and not to impose that need on others who aren't prepared to satisfy it.

A friendship is like a bank account. The more you put in, the more you can take out. I have friends who could be miserable and intolerable for weeks, and I'd let them stay at my place and do my best to help them get back to a good mental place. I wouldn't do that for strangers. With my friends I have a long and positive history, with so many good memories, experiences, and emotions, that they could draw from me for quite a while before I'd feel any sort of imposition.

And, of course, I feel the same way about my friends being there for me. I do my best to require little from others, but I have a group of close friends who would happily give me whatever support I needed if a situation arose.

But what happens when someone needs external

support but doesn't have close friendships? If he can't solve the problem himself, he ends up imposing on acquaintances. This is undesirable not just because it creates an imposition on the acquaintance, but also because it damages that relationship and decreases the likelihood of it growing into a meaningful friendship.

Reaching this goal requires a two-pronged approach: becoming self-reliant enough to only impose when necessary, and building such a sufficiently robust group of close friends that it's virtually impossible to overdraw on the friendship bank.

A person who is emotionally independent from acquaintances is most likely minimizing the impositions he creates on his friends, but is also making it very easy for new people to become his friends, since he asks nothing from them in the early stages of the friendship.

6. Be Able to Handle Oneself Socially in Any Situation

Similar to being able to relate to people across all social strata, it's also important to be able to handle oneself in any social situation that may arise. A good litmus test is to ask whether someone would feel comfortable introducing you to any of his friends or inviting you to any event.

For example, can you fend for yourself if you're dropped into a party? Can you strike up conversations with strangers and be a net positive without your friend introducing you and having to make sure that you're taken care of?

What if you're stuck talking with someone you don't really like? Can you be relied upon to be civil, not alienate them, and maybe even be a net positive to them? What if everyone in the party decides to go to a restaurant, and it's not the kind of food you want to eat? Will you go along and make the best of it?

This is so crucial because it directly affects the quality and quantity of introductions you receive, which will likely be a primary input into your social life. If the introducer can put you into any situation and expect that you will be an asset, even if you don't make a connection with the person he's introducing you to, you will get a lot more introductions.

Additionally, if you don't have to worry about the context of your interactions, only being comfortable in certain environments, that's one level of anxiety that won't be getting in between you and the people with whom you socialize.

7. Make People Like You More The Longer They Know You

First impressions are important, and we'll talk about them in detail, but it's your enduring impact that will determine how deep your friendships become. To have excellent friendships, and to maximize the opportunities for casual friends to turn into good friends, you must be the kind of person who becomes even better with more time.

We all know people who are the opposite. They're fun to have in big groups, because you can talk with them for a few minutes, but two hours with them would drive you crazy. It's tragic to see people like this sometimes, because you know that they're good people with good intentions and a lot to offer, but their social skills alienate others.

Ideally you want to feel as though anyone would like you, given enough time with you. This shouldn't really even be a reach-- it's a first step. Build up your social strengths, cut out weaknesses, and you're there.

If you do not have this now, you'll want to pay special attention to the sections of the book on eliminating social weaknesses. If you're a good person with some unique life experience, which I'm assuming you are, you're likable in the long term. If you find that people don't eagerly go the distance to become friends with you, it's probably because you're making some easily-correctable social mistakes that push them away.

Levels of Communication

The cable that comes into your home for TV has only two wires running through it. The cable itself is a rudimentary piece of technology that can be understood by anyone. But through this simple medium, hundreds of channels as well as access to the entire internet are transmitted. A lot is happening simultaneously.

This is very similar to how we communicate. Our words may seem very simple, but there are actually several different channels of communication being transmitted at the same time. To master social skills, you must be aware of these channels, be able to communicate effectively on them, and be able to understand what is being transmitted to you over them.

There are four main channels being communicated on at all times: content, meta, emotion, and status.

Content is what we think of when we talk about communication superficially. If you tell me that you're going to the store, the content channel is simply telling me that you are going to travel to the store.

The meta channel is the undercurrent of the conversation. It's the meaning behind the meaning-- the implication. If we had just been talking about how I wanted to eat brownies, and you're going to the store, the meta channel communication is that you're going to go get ingredients to make me brownies. Sometimes meta can be read in isolation, but it usually requires context.

The emotion channel is more of a passive signal than an active channel. Those of us who are not expert poker players are constantly leaking out our emotions as we speak. You could say, "I'm going to the store" in any number of tones and cadences. You could indicate that you were going to the store in resignation, because I wouldn't stop hounding you about making me brownies. You could indicate that you loved me, and that's why you were going to get ingredients to make me brownies. You could also reveal that you were frustrated, nervous, excited, or any other number of emotions.

And last, the status channel is constantly sending out clues about our relative status. If I were your boss and told you to go make brownies, you could say, "I'm going to the store" as an affirmation that you understood my command and were going to comply with it. You could also say it in a patronizing tone that indicates that you're going to do it because I'm so far below you that I'm incapable of doing such a basic task myself.

I'm going to the store. Five basic words, chosen at random, that could mean just about anything, even though the content doesn't change. If you weren't already awed at the power of communication, this just might do it. It's incredible how much can be conveyed simultaneously.

A master of communication must be able to have two major conversations (content and meta), while maintaining two minor conversations (emotion and status). This is no exaggeration. If someone were to transcribe the meta conversation between you and another person, it should be totally coherent. Same with the other two. If that conversation did not flow as smoothly as the content channel, you'd find that the conversation was frustrating to one or both of you, even if you couldn't identify why.

Each channel has its own strengths and weaknesses, so when it's important to convey something, you need to choose the right channel to focus on. I'll spare you a discussion on the content channel, since you're clearly able to understand it if you're able to read this book, but the other three channels deserve individual attention, especially since the most important aspects of conversation happen in the channels hidden behind the content channel.

Meta

The meta channel may be the most important of the four. It's where real discussions happen. In fact, sometimes you intentionally communicate incorrect information on the content channel, through sarcasm or joking, allowing your real message to come through on meta.

The key thing to understand about the meta channel is that it's running all the time. Nothing you say will be taken entirely at face value. People you speak with will always be wondering what you really mean.

Let's say that you suggested that a group go eat pizza. A couple people agree to do so, and then another person says, "I guess I could do pizza". What he's really communicating on the meta channel is that he is willing to conform to group consensus and go eat pizza, but that he'd rather eat somewhere else.

Now people answering after him can take that information into account when forming their own responses. If the next person says, "Pizza sounds good", he's actually communicating a strong preference for pizza. He's ignoring the meta message from the previous person. If he were less interested in pizza, the meta communication from the previous person gave him the opportunity to begin shifting opinion. He could have said, "I could do pizza, or something else."

Once everyone answers, you have a good idea of how everyone in the group feels about it, but you still have options. If people hesitantly agreed and communicated on the meta channel that they'd rather go somewhere else, you could have switched plans.

You might wonder what the point of this all is, especially if you're a very logical person. Certainly it would be easier to just communicate facts in the content channel and have no meta channel.

The point of the meta channel is that it allows for

shades of gray not afforded by the content channel. If the content channel is a lecture, the meta channel is a dance. It's pushing and pulling, circling and parrying. Imagine if someone said, "I'll eat at the pizza place, but I'd rather go somewhere else." That's exactly what our first person communicated on meta, but when it's in the content channel, it actually means something different. It's a much stronger disagreement, and is the beginning of a disharmonious decision-making process.

Communicating on the meta channel also allows people to save face. Let's say you met someone and really liked them. They said that they want to go see a Vermeer exhibit at a local museum. Their meta channel is a bit unclear. Maybe they're inviting you, or maybe they're not. You reply that you've also been wanting to see that same exhibit. Now you're communicating that you're not sure if it's an invitation, but that you'd like to go. If they aren't crazy about you, they can just start talking about Vermeer, and thus communicate that they don't want to go with you. You can continue to have a civil conversation and not feel insulted.

If you instead focus on the content channel and say, "Hmm... I'm not sure if you're inviting me or not, but I'd like to go," you put them in a very awkward position. This is the exact type of conversation that should happen over the meta channel so that neither person is made to feel bad.

Once you are really tuned into the meta channel, you

might feel as though you are in the matrix. Even when people aren't intending to communicate on the meta channel, you can infer their subcommunications. You understand not just the "what" of people are saying, but also the why, and you gain the power to have two complete conversations at the same time.

The first step to communicating on the meta channel is to constantly ask yourself why people are saying the things they say. Why did he choose that exact phrasing? Why didn't she say something else instead? Why share that information now? Come up with some ideas in your head, and check them later when you have more information. By making predictions and checking their accuracy later, you'll begin to calibrate your brain. When a prediction was off its mark, take the time to analyze and think about it.

Once you understand meta communication, you want to start shaping your own meta communication. What we say can be interpretend in many different ways, so you have to really craft what you say for the specific person you're with whom you're talking. Try to create a simulator in your brain where, as you consider what to say, you predict how the listener will react, and what meaning they'll assign to it. Think about what you'd like to communicate, and decide whether it's better to do it on the content channel or the meta channel. Which will make the other person feel more comfortable? Which will give you more options? Which gives them more options?

Sometimes when I read a non-fiction book, I decide

that no matter what, I'm going to at least make one change as a result. I hope for a big breakthrough, but even a small tip can make a book worth reading. If you were to decide to do that with this book, I'd recommend having that change be focused on communicating more through the meta channel.

Emotion

A lot of conversing is taking the other person on an emotional journey. You think about where they are emotionally, as well as where they want to be, and you use the emotional channel to guide them there, or keep them there if they want to stay in the same place.

For example, let's say you meet someone at a concert. They're excited and having fun, which is exactly why they are at the concert, so they want to maintain that state. If you initiate a serious talk about business, you are grossly miscommunicating on the emotional channel. Even if they really enjoy business and being serious, it's so inappropriate in this context that they'll retreat from the conversation.

On the other hand, you could probably talk about business in a really excited tone, and they'd engage with the conversation. The exact context would dictate whether it would work or not, but it's clear that it's a lot better than trying to be serious.

Consider someone who had a bad day and is frustrated. They probably want to shift to being happy and calm. You can slowly lead them in that direction by making the conversation increasingly positive. Maybe you'd start by matching their tone and asking them questions about the day, and then slowly bring some optimism to the conversation.

On the other hand, if someone were upset because they had a death in the family, though, they probably don't want to be happy. It just feels wrong. Maybe they want to feel understood and supported. You could communicate those things emotionally by listening, asking questions, and offering to do things to help.

Not every conversation is spiked with emotion, but there's usually some emotion there. If it's boredom, you've got to change that as soon as you can. If you're just getting to know someone, maybe you'd want to emotionally communicate a little bit of mystery about yourself as well as excitement about getting to know them. Be aware of the emotional tone of conversation and think about the directions you could move that emotion.

Status

There is an invisible hierarchy in every group of people from two on up. If a decision had to be made, who would make it? If there were a crisis, to whom would people in the group turn to solve it? Who has to be more careful about what they say?

Humans are hierarchical creatures. We want to know where we stand, not for vanity, but to inform how we speak and act.

I could propose any combination of your friends, and you could probably sketch out a hierarchy. Maybe it would be totally flat, everyone being a peer, but more likely there would be a leader or two who get spoken to with just a tiny bit more deference and take more responsibility for the group. Whatever the hierarchy, everyone in the group would probably unconsciously agree to it and act and speak accordingly.

When you join a new friend group, you want to understand the hierarchy. As an outsider, it's important to maintain the harmony of the group, and not disturb it. If you understand how the members relate to each other, that will be a lot easier to do. Even one on one, status is important. Understanding someone's status is understanding how they view their place in the world.

And, of course, you want to communicate your own status. Some people will treat everyone with respect, but others only treat people with respect if they demand it. So your default outgoing communication on the status channel with someone new should usually be that you deserve respect and are worth getting to know.

A lot of status is communicated nonverbally with body language and eye contact. Direct eye contact conveys high status universally. Taking up a lot of space with your body also conveys high status.

Talking about how high-status you are actually conveys low status. So does doing almost anything that is inappropriate in context. If you take up a lot of space where there's space to spare, you will appear to be high-status. If you take up a lot of space on a train where there are people who want to sit down, you just look insecure and try-hard.

Vocal tone also communicates a lot about status. Someone who talks slightly louder than average and with clarity will appear to be more important.

Instinctively reading status from the way people act and speak is consistent and accurate, which indicates that it's extremely difficult to fake. If you feel like someone is high status, they probably are. If you think they're overreaching and are trying to convince you that they're high status, they probably are faking.

For this reason, it's dangerous to try to fake your own status through body language and tonality. As you become more comfortable and confident, these aspects of communication will naturally change in a positive way.

However, much of status is about what you will and won't accept from yourself and others. That can't be faked, but it can be changed.

For example, many people will agree with higher status people as a blanket policy. Your boss says that he thinks the food at a restaurant is terrible, and you agree with him even though you think it's great. The "cool guy" at a party loves a song, and suddenly everyone likes it, too. This is a low status behavior that invites disrespect.

Disagreeing with everything is even worse, but expressing your own opinion in a clear and appropriate way conveys that you have the ability to think for yourself, even in the presence of strong outside influence. You will be given respect for doing this.

Another major changeable status indicator is whether you take responsibility or not. If you're at a restaurant and someone needs to speak to the waiter about moving some tables together, are you the one who does so? When a conversation is flagging, do you take the initiative and revive it? Ever-so-surprisingly, actually being a leader indicates to others that you are, in fact, a leader.

Be aware of what others are communicating on the status channel, and avoid mannerisms or habits that accidentally convey lower status. In general you should be communicating that you are a peer to people with whom you want to become friends. If you feel like someone is making an effort to appear higher status than you, it's sometimes worth taking action like speaking louder and taking up more space to place yourself a hair above them, only because they've indicated that status is important to them and that they respond to higher status.

Conveying Value Early And Fast

When you are introduced to someone or put into a social situation where people don't know you, your first goal should be to convey as quickly as possible what makes you interesting and worth knowing. It is, of course, important to get to know others and to do your part to make the interaction more interesting and fun for everyone else, but letting them know you is your first priority. First impressions are made quickly and endure as subconscious biases for a very long time.

People make decisions quickly, so you want to maximize your chances of them viewing you favorably. They share more of themselves with people they deem worthy of their friendship, and only on equal footing can you help improve the interaction.

The value that you convey must be true and authentic. That means that exaggerating is a bad idea. When people have few data points to judge you on, each one will be used and weighted heavily to mean more than it actually does. So if you exaggerate once or say something that doesn't really seem to jive with who you are, it will be noticed and held against you.

Worse than exaggerating is outright bragging. Any level of bragging will nullify anything positive you've managed to communicate. So the trick is to convey as much of yourself as possible without bragging.

For this reason, you'll want to focus less on what you've done and more on who you are. And you want this information to be second-order information, meaning that you want a reasonable person to infer attributes about you based on what you say.

For example, let's say you started a business and just did a million dollars in sales. That's something to be proud of, but there's no possible way to bring it up that won't make you seem like you're bragging. However, you could talk about different productivity strategies you have. People could then infer from those strategies that you're a motivated and productive person, which is a positive thing in almost any social circle.

Similarly, you wouldn't want to talk about how you travel to all sorts of exotic locations, but you could share a tip for getting seat upgrades or talk about a funny travel story you have. From those non-bragging and authentic stories, people will infer that you're adventurous and like to travel.

You can also convey value through asking questions. If someone else is an expert in an area, you could ask a question that presupposes a certain type of knowledge. If you flew airplanes, it would be inappropriate to come out and say, "Hey guys, I'm a pilot!" but you could ask someone who flew helicopters about specific differences between the two.

You'll notice that these alternatives are also more

valuable to the listener. They inform, entertain, or engage, rather than just impress. If you're not sure if you're bragging or not, don't say it. Bragging is extremely detrimental, and you'll have plenty of other opportunities to convey value.

The value you're trying to convey is attributes about yourself that make you an interesting and pleasant person. You want to build intrigue without conveying arrogance, and demonstrate that you are socially adept, non-needy, and will be an asset to the person or group with whom you're interacting.

A sense of humor is a huge source of value. Not everyone is funny, and not everyone has to be, but if you are a funny person, you can convey a lot of value with humor. Every social group enjoys laughing and having a good time. There are times where joking around isn't appropriate, but those times are usually not when you're first meeting someone. Even if a person or group thinks you have no value whatsoever except that you make them laugh, they'll still probably want you around.

Consider what about you makes you valuable as a friend, and whenever you're in a new social situation, think about which of your assets will most be appreciated by that group and work on conveying them. Do it early in the interaction and then move on to getting to know everyone else.

Eliminating Annoyance

Before you begin working on how to bring a lot to the table as a friend and a member of a friend group, it's important to work on eliminating behaviors which cause annoyance. None of us will completely succeed in eliminating all our annoying behaviors, but there's a certain threshold that must be crossed for people with other good options to choose you as a friend.

This is a harsh thing to say, but that doesn't make it untrue. Some of those you will most want to become friends with will already have a ton of good friends who are all competing for their time. If you have annoying habits, there's no guarantee that a new friend or acquaintance will be able to see past those habits and discover the great things about you.

A classic example is talking too much about things that the other person isn't interested in. There are guidelines to follow on how much of the conversation should be you listening versus you speaking, but in general volume alone won't make or break an interaction. After all, even if you prefer being the one to talk, if I'm revealing interesting discoveries about subjects that matter to you, you're unlikely to want me to stop.

But if I'm talking about my ambitions as a marathoner, and you have no interest in running, your capacity to enjoyably listen to me is limited.

Another very common annoying habit is making bad

jokes. No one thinks that they make bad jokes, but everyone knows some people that do, so there's an obvious disconnect. Some people consistently make bad jokes, and don't realize it. You might be one of these people.

Both of these are undesirable traits, not because you're malicious or because they imply something bad about you, but because they create an unnecessary imposition on the other person, and require him to either deceive you or be rude.

If you talk too much to me about subjects in which I have no interest, I must be polite, listen, and feign interest. The only alternative is for me to be rude, either by changing the subject as unabruptly as I can manage, or by telling you I'm not interested. Some people are so oblivious about overtalking that they won't pick up on any subtle cues.

If your jokes are bad, you again force me to either deceive you by laughing, or to not laugh and make you aware that your jokes aren't funny. In either scenario, you've placed an awkward imposition upon me, making me less comfortable, less interested in the conversation, and more motivated to exit.

Identifying annoying habits is more difficult than eliminating them. Often awareness creates enough social pressure to at least dampen the annoying habit. If you have a friend or family member who is willing to be completely honest with you, you can ask them what annoying habits you have. Don't ask if you have any, just assume that you do, and ask what they are. This saves your friend the awkward step of revealing to you that you have some.

Think about how often you'd be wrong when pointing out someone else's annoying habit. Probably rarely to never, so when someone gives you that sort of feedback, assume that they are correct.

You will have to find some annoying habits on your own, though. The biggest red flag is when you are consistently getting reactions that differ from those you expect. You make a joke, and the laughter is muted. You talk about something that's really interesting to you, but you see eyes wander and notice that your listeners don't ask any clarifying questions.

These are just two examples of many. Others include overuse of certain words, unnecessary hand gestures, not making eye contact, and not listening.

Don't Talk Too Much

When you begin a conversation with a new person, you should have a loose default of doing all or most of the talking. If the person isn't socially adept and can't think of things to say, it won't be a problem, since you'll fill any silence with interesting stories, questions, and observations.

Eventually you want to transition to a lower ratio, preferably fifty-fifty. If you have someone who is really shy, you may always be at sixty or seventy percent, but greater than that is a lecture, not a conversation, and it's very likely the other person will become frustrated.

Most people are polite and will generally allow you to steamroll them socially and dominate the conversation. However, that doesn't mean that it's a good thing to do. This leads to situations where you'll feel like a conversation went really well, but then the other person doesn't ever seem to want to hang out.

So how do you know if you're overtalking or if the other person is just shy? There are several signs that you should be constantly looking out for if you're speaking more than fifty percent of the time.

The first warning sign is if you know the other person is an extrovert and likes to talk. If he hasn't asked you to explain something and you're talking more than fifty percent of the time, you're making a mistake.

If the other person gives short answers or the same answer repeatedly, he is not interested in the conversation. For example, if his input is "yeah" or "nice", but he never invests in a longer answer, he's probably hoping that you'll stop talking. An interesting discussion will probably invite follow-up questions or a contrasting point of view. If you don't get either of those things, be on guard.

Maybe the biggest warning sign is if someone never asks you questions. People ask questions when they want to hear more from you, and stop asking questions when they want less. If you never get questions, that probably means the other person is concerned that you won't stop talking if you start answering.

As a general rule, never over-explain. If you're talking about something intellectual, do the bare minimum amount of explanation. As soon as someone nods or agrees with something you say, move on to your next point. When explaining, question and answer is the ideal format. It allows the person receiving the information to get exactly the information he needs, in the depth he prefers, and it keeps the provider of the information confident that his input is valued.

If you need to share a long story or provide and involved explanation, put in lots of pauses. The best stories and explanations leave the listener rapt, afraid to speak and miss something. If the silences aren't filled, you can be sure that the person wants to hear what you have to say. If he asks questions, that's equally good. But if he changes the subject or decreases the depth of the conversation, he's probably looking for a way out.

It's perfectly fine to love talking, but remember that you won't really be heard unless the other person is receptive. Use natural signals to understand where his interest level lies, and change your communication to suit. Over a longer time span, couple that skill with practicing telling good stories in a compelling way, to minimize people feeling like you're talking for too long.

Recalibrate for Responses

As you're speaking with someone, you should intently gauge their responses. This isn't to feed your ego or to beat yourself up, but to enable you to take responsibility for the conversation and to give the other person the experience that they want.

While gauging, it's important to grade on a sliding scale that takes into account the context and setting of the conversation. For example, if someone was introduced to you at a mutual friend's party, it is very likely that they will act more interested in your conversation than they are. So if it feels like they're a five on a scale from one to ten of interest, that may actually be a zero, plus five points of politeness.

In that situation, you'd be wise to cut off a story you were telling and see if they ask you to continue. If they don't, their interest level was lower than it appeared. If they do ask you to continue, then they were interested after all. Sometimes you can't tell, because a five and zero may look exactly the same.

And, of course, there are times when the scale works the other way. Some people show very little emotion, or would be acting inappropriately showing too much enthusiasm. An acquaintance's girlfriend might blunt her responses to avoid giving the impression of flirting with you, so you could rightly assume that she was more interested in topics you brought up than she appeared to be.

This is important because conversations should create a feedback loop. You make a statement, tell a story, or ask a question, and then you gauge the response. How well-received that statement or question was should inform your future decisions. Too often people forget to adjust their assessments based on external factors and will continue talking about something boring because the other person is being polite. While it can be fun to talk about topics you're interested in, you're doing more bad than good if the other person isn't interested in the topic.

Drop Conversational Hooks

Much of social skills is creating the experience that the other person wants, and making it as effortless and natural as possible. A big part of this is making sure that the topics you cover are topics about which the other person wants to talk.

The easiest way to do this is to drop conversational hooks and allow the other person to pick up on those that hold his interest. This is not a one-time strategy, but a framework to use for conversations on an ongoing basis.

One of the most awkward parts of socializing, especially with someone new, is coming up with conversational topics. If your counterpart feels like they have to rack their brain to come up with things to talk about, they will have a strong motivation to leave the conversation.

In an ideal situation you provide them with a choice of topics to talk about, in a natural way, and keep adding to that list as you continue. Instead of that panic felt when the topics run out, your partner will feel like there's so much to talk about and not enough time to get it all in. That's a much better problem to have.

The general idea is that you tell one story and lace it with as many hints about other stories and conversations as possible. For example:

"Back when I lived in California, I had this friend who lived on an Icelandic car ferry. We were working on a project together, and were having an argument about whether we should hire someone or not..."

The story may be about how you decided whether or not to hire someone, but there are several topical hooks that have been dropped. You could talk about California, living on a boat, Iceland, or the project you were working on. This often leads to chance overlaps, like, "I used to live in San Francisco. Where did you live?"

This also provides the other person with a very convenient way to stop your story if they're not that interested. It's a game of constant escalation of interest, allowing them to hop through your topics until one is so interesting that it becomes a real conversation. At the same time, it doesn't burden them with the responsibility of coming up with the topic themselves.

Early in a relationship, a subgoal of any conversation is to give as much accurate information about yourself as possible. The more context someone has, the more they'll get out of every bit of information you give them. By dropping hooks, even if they're not picked up, you provide more points to connect about you.

Be careful to avoid bragging when dropping hooks. The hooks should always be neutral or slightly positive things, never huge accomplishments.

Leading someone to a topic that makes you look really good is a dangerous thing to do, as it makes it look as though you were trying to brag. If you must do it, you want to leave the least bragging hook possible. So you would never say, "Back when I ran a marathon", but you could say, "Back when I was running".

And don't worry when your hooks aren't being picked up. There are a million different reasons that could be happening, and only one of them is that you're a boring person with no interesting topics. Much more likely is that they don't want to switch the subject or that they haven't yet heard a hook where they can add anything interesting.

Stories

Books like How To Win Friends and Influence People by Dale Carnegie place a strong emphasis on asking questions and listening to the other person. This is a critical part of social skills, but so is being able to convey who you are. Friendships are formed when people feel good emotionally, which comes from being asked questions, being listened to, and being interested in the other person. Your primary tool for conveying who you are and making people interested is through your stories.

When evaluating others, we are always looking for proof of claims. I can recite some memorized facts to give the impression that I'm smart, but it's not proof. Some experts believe that a sense of humor is attractive because it is proof of intelligence that can't be faked. It takes brainpower to make unusual connections, read the other person, and deliver a few sentences to make them laugh. You can't just memorize jokes to do this, you have to be able to improvise. That's where the proof lies.

If I tell you that I'm interesting, smart, kind, and a good friend, that doesn't really carry much weight. Maybe you'll believe me, or maybe you'll suspect that I'm just saying those things even though they're not actually true.

A common interview technique, in lieu of asking people whether they have desirable attributes, is to ask them to tell a story about a time they exhibited one of the attributes for which you're selecting. If you ask someone if they react well in a crisis, the answer is always yes, but asking them them to tell you about a crisis that they resolved successfully will prove it.

While it's not impossible to make up a story, it's significantly harder, and therefore more convincing, than just saying "yes". Telling true stories is important because it's your primary method of conveying who you are in a way that is easy to absorb and remember, and can be believed by the other person.

If there's a single skill I can recommend that you spend time on, it's the art of telling a story. It provides you with a way to entertain your friends, control the mood of an interaction, and efficiently convey who you are.

How to Tell a Story

Most people tell stories for the wrong reasons. They do it because it's fun, because they want to impress the other person, or even just because there's dead time that needs to be filled. If you tell stories with these goals, your stories won't necessarily be creating much of a positive experience for the other person.

Your goal when telling a story is to convey something noteworthy about yourself in a way that is enjoyable to the other party or parties. You want for it to be a good time for them, and for it to reflect well upon you. This should be your primary motivation when you begin to tell a story.

When someone is getting to know you, they are trying to understand your character and your status. Who are you, and how do you fit into the world they know? These questions are answered not so much by the main arc of the story, but by the arc's shadow. It's the small details of the story that will illustrate who you are.

You could have a story that, when compressed to a single sentence, makes you look bad. For example: "I tried to chat up the star of my favorite childhood TV show while she was on a double date, but failed miserably." On the surface that sounds like a bad story to tell. It's fine for people to find out your flaws and mistakes, but if you are offering up a story, it should be one that says positive things about you.

The details determine whether the story actually shows you in a positive or negative light. For example, did I react calmly when faced with the high-pressure situation of approaching the star on a double date? Was she intrigued and amused, even though her date was rude? Did I display social awareness? Did I deal with my failure gracefully and treat it as a fun little diversion?

Think about the opposite. I could have succeeded and looked glorious in a sentence, but looked like an idiot in the details. Maybe she gave me her number because I was annoying her, but I didn't notice that. Maybe I'm just a little too proud about the whole thing.

When someone's getting to know you, and you want to become friends with them, choose a story where the details highlight your positive attributes. Don't make stories up, don't change them to be positive, just pick the stories that convey what you're hoping to convey.

Hollywood movies are mostly similar in structure, but we keep watching them. More than that, we're engrossed in the stories and buy into the tension and surprises they contain. There's a very standard pattern that works, and they mold the story they want to tell to that structure. Movie studios have done the research, but found that there's virtually no point in coming up with new structures, because the standard one works so well.

When telling a story, you should have three primary phases in order: the setup, the buildup, and the payoff. Practice telling every story according to this format so that it becomes an ingrained pattern in your mind, and only once mastered consider telling stories that don't fit that format.

Keep the setup very short, giving only the minimum amount of information needed so that the story makes sense. You might set the time the story took place, the location, a brief mention of the characters, and any relevant emotional cues. For example: "This was three years ago, in Texas. Two close friends from college and I were standing in front of a cave we'd never seen before."

You might describe the friends a bit more, or some relevant details about the cave, but by and large the setup part of your story should be very concise. This is because there is no tension or drama in the setting, and those are the elements that keep people interested in the story. Use the setup to transport the listener or listeners into the story.

The biggest mistake that people make in the setup is that they include far too many details. Always err on the side of too few and trust your audience to ask if something is not clear. And never go on tangents. If one is warranted, make a very brief mention of it as a hook, and then move on immediately.

The buildup is the variable length portion of the story. Any given story will have a relatively short setup and payoff, but the buildup could be any length. The buildup tells the facts of the story, in such a way as to build the tension and keep the listener engaged. It should be a constantly escalating journey that you take your listener on.

This is also the part of the story that you never tell the same way twice. That's because it should be dynamic, based on the reaction of your listeners. If they are rapt and hanging on your every word, you can draw the story out longer, ratcheting up the tension. The best way to do that is to tell the story in such a way that your friends will mentally try to guess what happens next, but constantly be hit with surprises. If they're bored or not fully engaging with the story, you keep the buildup quick.

"... so the night finally came when we decided to do the heist. From our designated positions, we slowly crept into place. I was in front, so I put my hand on the doorknob and twisted. It was unlocked..."

Here you can actually add more details, especially emotional ones, that may have bored people during the setup. This is possible because it prolongs the drama. But the details must be relevant.

"... at this point, my heart was pounding. I thought back to the steps that got me here, and it all made sense, but I couldn't believe that I was actually about to commit a heist. And I knew that as soon as I opened the door, there was no turning back."

These details don't add any better understanding to the story, but they do take the reader on an emotional journey. If they were engrossed in the story, you'd add more of these sorts of details. If they weren't that interested, you'd cut most of them.

Last comes the payoff, which must resolve the story in one way or another and hopefully include some sort of revelation. In my heist example, you'd talk about how you got caught, or got cold feet, or succeeded in doing the heist. The goal with the payoff is to either release all of the tension created by the buildup, or to sidestep in such a way that all of the tension was unnecessary.

The payoff is the big moment in the story, and it's a natural high point. It's your cue to exit the story and stop talking. If you keep talking, you lessen the impact of the story and ruin it. But if you consistently end stories with a strong payoff, people will want to hear more of your stories. They've trusted you with their attention, and you've respected it by giving the minimum background, an exciting buildup, and a satisfying payoff at the end.

To illustrate, a quick story, segmented.

Background

A couple years ago I was on a date at a restaurant called Real Food Daily in West Hollywood. It's this hip vegan place with really good food, and you always see celebrities there because being vegan is trendy.

I'm sitting there with my back to the wall, looking at the restaurant behind the girl I'm on a date with, and I see Jay-Z.

Buildup

Now, I'm a huge Jay-Z fan. Like, for three years I listened to no other artists, and I wrecked a date in a ball of flames when I found out she'd gone on a date with Jay-Z and I couldn't stop talking about it.

And, almost immediately, I begin to wreck another

date. I completely zone out everything she's saying, focusing only on Jay-Z. My favorite musician is right there, about fifteen feet away from me. I have to say something to him.

But first, I have to make sure it's really him. I text a friend and ask him to see if he can search the internet to figure out where Jay-Z is. And, sure enough, he's in LA, in between two shows.

Now I'm really excited. This is really happening. At this point, I'm barely giving coherent responses to my date. I'm focusing 100% on Jay-Z, trying to plan out everything I'll say to him. I'm nervous like I haven't been in years.

I don't want to be rude and bother him while he's eating, though, so I decide that I'll wait until he leaves. I'll plan what to say, be ready, and then follow him outside and talk to him. Not a perfect plan, but this is a crazy opportunity, and I'm not going to let it go to waste.

Finally, he gets up. I wait a second, then follow him outside, heart pounding. I go over my lines in my head, ready to act really calm and cool. He goes out the door, and I follow him.

I muster up my courage and tap him on the shoulder. "Excuse me, Mr. Carter?" Slowly, he turns around and looks at me.

Payoff

Turns out it wasn't Jay-Z. It was just a guy who looked like him.

Have Lots of Stories

Stories are best when they are brought up in context. That context can be time-based ("Guess what happened to me just now?") or topic-based. You'll notice that stand-up comedians have two standard segues. One is to say, "Yesterday I _____", and the other is "Speaking of _____". The former makes a story relevant based on the time it happened, and the other makes it relevant due to the topic.

Comedians are always lying about when things happened. This is expected, because they're comics, but you should not do the same. For that reason, most of your stories will have to be topically relevant.

The key to having topically relevant stories is to have a lot of stories and to know what they are. I'd estimate that I have about two hundred good stories, across different topics. Some are funny, some are inspiring, some are sad, some are tense and awkward.

Having so many stories across topics as well as emotional states gives me a lot of maneuverability. For just about any topic that's brought up, I have at least one story I can contribute. Across topics that are popular amongst people I'm interested in getting to know, I might have several stories, each with a different tone.

That means that I can either match the tone of the conversation, or I can shift it by telling a story with a tone that I think is more conducive to the group dynamic.

I briefly took violin lessons. My teacher had this beautiful violin that I always wanted to play, but I never asked because I figured he'd just say no. We'd play the same piece, and I'd admire how rich his violin sounded. I wanted to play it so that I could hear myself make those same beautiful sounds. One day, he forgot to bring his violin to our lesson. He apologized, but said that he'd just play mine to demonstrate. He did that, and I was shocked-- it sounded exactly like his violin. It turns out the instrument didn't matter all that much.

The same is true of telling stories. People often incorrectly assume that they need amazing subject matter to tell a good story. That's always a nice bonus if you happen to have a good subject, but the skill of storytelling is what's really important. I just told you a story about how my violin teacher played my violin instead of his-- not exactly blockbuster story fodder, but it can be made interesting.

You already have plenty of material for stories. To practice telling stories I used to relate my trips to the grocery store to people, and I'm sure you've done more interesting things that grocery shopping. The key is to learn how to tell a good story so that more of the things that occur in your life can be told in an interesting manner.

If you don't feel like you have a lot of interesting stories, a good exercise is to take a sheet of paper and write the letters of the alphabet down the left side. Then come up with a short description of a story that begins with each letter. So mine might be A- Alaskan Motorcycle Trip B- Bank Robbery C- Crashed Motorcycle, all the way down to Z.

The simple act of racking your brain to come up with twenty-six stories is valuable. You could throw away the paper afterwards and still benefit from the exercise, just because it makes you realize how many stories you have. But you can also go a step further and memorize the list. Then when an awkward lull comes in a conversation, you quickly run through the list and tell the most relevant one.

By defining those twenty-six stories, you'll also be more likely to tell them repeatedly to different people. By doing that you'll be able to refine the stories and make them better.

Confidence is an important part of social skills and nearly impossible to fake convincingly. One way to gain confidence is to know that you have a repertoire of stories that you have told before to good effect and can call upon any time you feel like you don't know what to say.

Tell Stories About Your Friends that Make Them Look Good

There's a range of stories that you can tell about yourself, but there's a much wider range that you can tell about your friends. Some stories make you look so good that to tell them would come across as outright bragging. The only good way you can tell those stories is if someone insists, which happens rarely. However, if you know stories like that about your friends, you can tell them and then you both look good.

Your friend looks good because you're telling a story about him in which he shines. But he also looks good because his friend thinks highly enough him to prop him up. In addition, you look good because you are secure enough to make your friend look good rather than toot your own horn.

This concept also applies to interesting stories that wouldn't necessarily be construed as bragging, but are so out of context that they wouldn't otherwise come up. My friend Olivia, one of the most socially savvy people I know, always asks me to tell my story about trying to buy a pet penguin whenever she introduces me to new people. She's heard the story a million times but she knows that it will entertain her friends and will define who I am a little bit to them.

On the other hand, you should never tell stories that make your friends look bad. It's fine to expose their quirks, but if they messed something up, you'd never want to talk about that, even if it was a funny story. By doing that your friend looks bad, but you also look bad for putting down your friend. Besides, if someone's your friend, you should have enough good stories about them that there's never any occasion to tell stories that make them look bad, right?

Keep Stories in Reserve

A common source of social anxiety is the worry of running out of things to say. A long silence is no big deal between two close friends, but when you first meet someone, an awkward silence can be enough to cause one person to end the conversation. We have a subconscious understanding of this, and it can manifest itself as fear, which, unfortunately, makes it even harder to come up with things to say.

The simple answer is to always have stories in reserve. Before you go to a party with friends or a social event, think of one or two stories. They should be stories that you've told a million times and can tell without a lot of conscious thought. Then make it a goal to not tell those stories.

That leaves you with the motivation to rack your brain and come up with a good question or story when there's a pause, but you won't feel panicked, because you'll always have those stories in reserve. This makes it easier to come up with things to say in the conversation, but gives you good backups.

You might think about keeping questions in reserve, but that's not as effective. A story that you've told a many times will allow you, while you tell it, to think about the conversation and where to take it. Telling the story won't use all of your processing power, so you can use the spare brain cycles to plan.

A story is also more likely to lead to further conversation if you drop hooks in it, and it can make the person slightly more interested in you, so that they'll become more invested in keeping the conversation going. You might feel like you're going to have to use both of your stories in a row, but it almost always just takes one, and then the conversational flow solidifies, especially if you drop some hooks in it.

It's also a good idea to reserve some of your very best stories on a larger scale. Let's say that you have five stories, your best five, that are interesting to nearly everyone and each reveals a different side of you. Consider limiting yourself to telling just one per social interaction with someone.

Part of the fun of getting to know someone is unraveling their layers and learning more about them each time you spend time together. It's a process of mutual exploration that is satisfying and exciting to both people. If you tell all of your best stories all at once, you risk flaring out. You seem really interesting at first, and then the next time you meet up, you're trying to compete with your five most interesting stories. This opens up the door for the other person to think that maybe they had you wrong-- maybe you aren't that interesting.

If you save some stories and the other person gets to discover a new one each time for the first few times you hang out, you will reaffirm that you are interesting and worth getting to know. By the time you get through them, you'll be beyond the point of trying to be interesting, and will have a strong human connection.

Make the Other Person Comfortable

A key element to a good conversation is for both people to feel comfortable. Uncomfortable people clam up, leave the conversation, or say what they think the other person wants to hear rather than what they believe. People who are comfortable want the conversation to go on longer and invest more in it, making themselves vulnerable and talking about real things. Any good conversation you've ever had has involved a comfortable counterpart.

The first part of the formula is to make sure not just that the other person is physically comfortable, but that you are equally comfortable.

Imagine someone is sitting in an armchair and you are standing in front of them. Even though they are physically comfortable, your discomfort will make them mentally uncomfortable. It's okay to start a conversation like this, but you have to adapt quickly, either by sitting down or getting them to stand up with you. Both of you sitting is better than one sitting and one standing, but both standing is better than one person sitting.

Next, you want to adjust physical proximity. You want to be close enough to hear each other, but far enough that the other person doesn't feel encroached upon. Look to body language to determine how comfortable they are. If they are facing you with their body and face, then you are an appropriate distance. If they are turned away from you, this is a sign that you are too close.

Different cultures and relationship roles have different standards for physical proximity. You can be close to a family member or good friend, but probably shouldn't be so close to someone you've just met in business. Physical proximity can be changed on the fly, so play with it and watch the other person's reaction.

The other important comfort factor is how at ease the other person feels expressing himself. You can tell a good friend something controversial and it won't affect his opinion of you. But what about someone new? You never know if they'll shut down the conversation just because you disagree. So people stay guarded and don't invest in the conversation until they're comfortable.

A good shortcut to expressive comfort is to pleasantly disagree with the other person. Showing that you are listening but not judging is a great way to make them feel comfortable. For example, let's say they express a relatively safe opinion with which you disagree. You can say something like, "I've always thought the opposite, actually, but that's really interesting."

This gives a signal that you are comfortable with disagreement. They should then feel more open to sharing increasingly personal views, and having conversations that involve disagreement.

If you don't want to wait for them to share an opinion,

you can also offer one independently, but frame it in such a way that it's obvious that you don't judge people who think differently. For example, "I know not everyone agrees, but I've always thought _____. Who knows if I'm right or not, but it makes sense to me."

You shouldn't disclaim everything you say like that, but the first one or two controversial things you say could benefit from it. And it's a good idea to do this, even if you have non-controversial things you could say instead. In many situations, like when first getting to know someone, a good goal is to increase the depth of the conversation as quickly as possible.

As you speak with someone, constantly monitor their comfort level. Are they making eye contact? Do they laugh easily? Can they offer an opinion without feeling like they need to disclaim it? Are they focused on you, or are they looking away? People often misread discomfort as disinterest, but they're two very different things. If there are warning signs of discomfort, aim to relieve it before assuming it is disinterest.

Always Give the Other Person an Out

Teasing and banter are a valuable part of communication. They make people feel comfortable with each other, create a game that's fun to be a part of, and allow each person the opportunity to display their sense of humor and wit. Any interaction that has both people laughing is probably one that's moving the friendship in the right direction.

There is an important rule that must be observed during all conversations, especially those involving banter: always give the other person an out.

If you jokingly make fun of someone, you want there to be a clear retort that they can make to get you back. In reality, you should be joking for two, coming up with a way to tease the other person, but also having in mind at least one way they could tease you back.

For example, let's say you jokingly make fun of someone's cooking, even though it's good. It would be best if you had cooked something recently that was a total disaster, so that they could instantly say something like, "Oh yeah? You mean like when you tried to cook spaghetti?"

You won't always be left with outs, so you either laugh it off and show that you don't take yourself too seriously, or you scramble and come up with one of your own. Either way is good. Like many concepts in the book, you want to create an unfair playing field tilted towards the other person. You take responsibility for conversations, but never require them to take responsibility. You leave them outs, but don't count on them doing the same.

Besides having a way to get you back, the other person must not take damage from your jab. If he was sensitive about his cooking, you'd never want to joke about it. As a rule, you don't tease someone about something unless they have no reason to take offense to it. Otherwise your out that you leave them is only a false one.

Giving people outs extends beyond just joking around. Imagine that you're setting up a time to hang out and the conversation begins like this:

You: "Hey, want to hang out?"

Friend: "Sounds good. How about Friday?"

You: "Actually I'm busy Friday."

Friend: "Saturday, then?"

Let's say that you're busy on Saturday as well. If you just say that you're busy, you are essentially leaving your friend with no outs. His options are to suggest a third day and feel like he's really overextending himself, or to give up trying to hang out.

Better would have been to suggest a different day right up front:

Friend: "Sounds good. How about Friday?"

You: "Actually, I'm busy then. Does Sunday work for you?"

Now your friend doesn't have to put himself in an awkward position by continually suggesting days, only to be shut down by you.

The general principle is that for anything you say, there must be an appropriate response that your friend can make that makes him look good. He won't always come up with the same one that you think of, or even come up with one at all, but the opportunity must exist.

If you provide an out which your friend fails to take, and he is now in an awkward spot, you can bring it up yourself. For example, in the banter example, you could pause and say, "But hey... at least it wasn't like that pasta I tried to cook last week!"

No matter who you are or what your conversational style is, people want to feel good when they talk to you. That could be because you're in an interesting conversation, because you're complimenting them, or because you're bantering back and forth and they're never been backed into a corner.

Eye Contact

Short and sweet-- always make eye contact. In every conversation you have, you should maintain eye contact eighty percent of the time or more. Over ninety percent of the time is better. Studies show that, while controlling for other variables, eye contact causes people to like and trust each other more.

Eye contact indicates that the person you're speaking with has your full attention and is important to you. If those two things aren't true, it's probably better not to have the conversation in the first place. Not making eye contact is dismissive and rude. Look away to think or pause, but when you are speaking or the other person is speaking, you should look into their eyes.

You probably already do this, so I won't belabor the point. But I've met people who make almost no eye contact, and it's extremely uncomfortable talking with them.

Be Easily Distracted During Your Own Stories, But Not Theirs

There's nothing better than hearing a great story, and almost nothing worse than being stuck listening to a bad story that just won't end. For that reason, you want to make sure that your stories last a long time if the other person is really into them and are cut short if they aren't interested.

The easiest way to do this is to be easily distracted whenever you're telling a story, even if you think it's the best story you have.

If you can find a way to just stop talking, maybe because someone has interrupted your conversation or because the waiter has brought your food, take that opportunity and never bring the story back up. Just assume that it's dead. If your friend interrupts you, switch to whatever they're talking about.

If the other person is interested, they will bring the topic back up. No one is too shy to ask to hear the rest of a really interesting story. And if they're not interested, the story dies. That's frustrating sometimes, because it's fun to tell stories, but telling someone a story they aren't interested in hearing is always a negative.

As you do this, pay attention to which stories never get brought back from the dead, and bias yourself towards not telling them to other people. Some stories are good, some are duds, and some will only be enjoyed by certain people. It's good to know which are which.

The better you know someone, the less you have to drop your stories. Eventually you know people well enough to make intelligent predictions about which stories they'll enjoy and which they won't. So most stories you'll just tell the whole way through. If you detect even a whiff of disinterest, you can drop the story gracefully.

On the other hand, always allow others to finish their stories, even if they're boring. You can break this rule for very close friends who appreciate blunt criticism, but that will be a very small minority of the people with whom you interact.

Your goals in a conversation are to make sure that the other person enjoys themselves, to allow them to learn about you, and for you to learn about them. By allowing them to tell a story that's not all that interesting, you are letting them enjoy themselves, and you're also learning about them, even if it's in a tedious format.

Crossing the Line

In any given social situation, there's a bounding line that dictates what's polite and what's too intimate. This line is defined by the relationship between the people in the conversation. For example, you could tell your best friend that he's gaining weight and should hit the gym, but you would never say that to a stranger.

Another example is the tone and texture of language used. With a new contact in a professional setting, profanity, certain colloquialisms, or slang would be outside the line.

Some people routinely cross this line, but they are very few. Usually the breaches are along the lines of slang or profanity, rather than truly offending someone. On the other hand, I'd contend that the vast majority of people draw the line too tightly.

Friendships deepen with voluntary increases in intimacy. There's a wag the dog sort of effect where deepening friendships cause intimacy to increase, but it also works in reverse.

When two people begin communicating, both are, among other things, trying not to look foolish. Safe opinions and pleasantries never make someone look like a fool, so very often they are the topics that people stick to when they aren't well acquainted.

As in many life situations, there's a big difference

between "playing not to lose" and "playing to win". You can go through your entire life without ever giving anyone a reason to dislike you, but still not make a single close friend. On the other hand, you can give a lot of people reasons to not like you and still create a great group of friends with other people.

This doesn't mean that you want to offend people or make people not like you, only that it can be worth risking "friend rejection" if that strategy wins you more good friends in the end. In practice, this means that you want to get very close to the line, possibly crossing it in small steps from time to time.

One way to cross the line a little bit is to tease the other person. Nothing actually offensive, but something that you might say to a close friend. Doing this not only breaks a barrier and moves you closer to friendship, but it also allows the other person to act friendlier towards you. The old line is now within the new one, so he can safely be more friendly without putting himself at risk of seeming foolish.

One of my favorite examples from my own life is when I was seated on a cruise ship next to an older English couple and two younger Romanian girls. It was our first night sitting together, and the talk was all superficial chit-chat. The English man took a piece of bread and offered it to the Romanians. As they reached to take it, I put out my hand to stop them and said, "Oh, no.... Romanians don't eat bread."

On its own, this isn't a very funny joke. But I knew

that I could cross that line and get away with it, and the tension of me crossing the line caused everyone to laugh. That's the kind of joking around you'd do amongst friends, and the feeling of the dinner immediately changed to casual and friendly. From then on, we all joked around together every night.

You can also cross the line by revealing something personal, like a struggle you're going through or something embarrassing that happened. This serves the same purpose: to act more like friends, and to allow the other person the opportunity to reveal something about himself.

If you are not very confident in your ability to assess where the line is, it's best to approach it gradually and in measured steps. Test the waters and, if the response is good, push even further. If you cross too far and make someone uncomfortable, you've probably only made them slightly uncomfortable, from which you can easily recover.

As illustrated in the Romanian bread example, crossing the line is at least as effective in group settings as it is one-on-one. In a group it is harder to cross the line, so most people will be too reserved to do it. Sometimes two people who could be quite friendly in a one-on-one setting will act formally when surrounded by others. Like so many other techniques in this book, you want to take responsibility for everyone else's experience and put yourself out there by being the one to cross it. Very often you'll find that everyone gets significantly more comfortable as soon as you do. You've set a new friendly tone for the interaction that everyone tacitly agrees to by not being offended.

Again, it's important to stress that this does not mean that you want to be obnoxious or just run across lines. The takeaway should be that a line does exist, but that it's further out than most people are typically willing to go, and by crossing it very slightly you actually endear people to you and make the conversation more friendly.

Involve Everyone

When you're speaking in a group situation, you are assuming a lot of responsibility. You are taking the attention and time of several different people, and are implicitly promising them that what you fill that time with will be worthwhile. Or at least you should be doing that-- if you're not, then you're wasting people's time.

There are a lot of ways to fill that time meaningfully. You could be asking questions to begin an interesting discussion, you could be telling a great story, or you could be sharing some insight into something that you've learned recently.

There are also a lot of ways to waste that time and attention. I ate dinner with a group once, where one guy was absolutely intent on relating his history of purchases at airport duty free shops. Seriously, "Well, in Heathrow, I bought a liter of Cuantro. It was only ten pounds!" for dozens of minutes.

Even if some people were interested in his duty free stories, he made a critical mistake. He didn't involve everyone.

When you're taking conversational responsibility of a group, it is your obligation to make sure that everyone is involved in the discussion. Not actively, necessarily, but everyone must be interested in what you're talking about.

That means that you make eye contact with everyone to personally connect with them. It also means that you don't go on about duty free purchases with a group of people that don't drink. And it means that if someone is losing interest, you either ask them a question to reengage or change the topic to something that everyone would be interested in.

You may be tempted to focus only on the people within the group in whom you're most interested. You'll go to a party, connect with one person, and during a group conversation you'll focus on them because they're the one you like the most.

This is a mistake, though. You have to remember that everyone in a group setting is there for a reason. Even if you don't like Bob, someone there does. Maybe it's one of the people you like the most. If Bob is having a bad time, he may disrupt the conversation, or someone who really likes him may notice that he's not enjoying the conversation and then they'll become disengaged.

As you speak, or even as others are speaking, look around the group and try to guess how interested they are in the current topic. For most it will be obvious, but if you do this as a habit, even the harder to read ones will become more obvious. When you notice that someone is disengaged, think about what might bring them back in.

The first consideration when considering how to bring someone back in is to assess whether they prefer listening or speaking. Some people love to be in the spotlight, while others prefer to listen, as long as the conversation is interesting.

If the person prefers to speak, try asking their opinion. A good generic way to do this is to say something like, "Jean, you always have interesting takes on these sorts of topics, what do you think?"

Unless the topic is very far from their interests, this will engage almost anyone. When a conversation makes someone feel important, the conversation then feels more important to them. Even if they quickly give an opinion and then the conversation continues, they will be more engaged because they've invested in it.

If the disengaged person is more of a listener, the solution isn't quite as easy. If you're in the middle of telling a story, you might consider speeding it up and getting to the next topic. If several people are disengaged, you might cut the story and just skip to the next one. Another tactic is to make the story, or part of the story, relevant to the other person. You could say something like, "We were in Berlin, where I think you lived for a while, right, Katy?" This one sentence makes the story relevant and can increase Katy's engagement.

In a large group, you may not really be able to keep everyone engaged all of the time. People have varying levels of interest in different topics and types of socialization. What's even more important is to make sure people are not socially excluded across periods of time longer than a single story.

I frequently run into another common mistake when I'm in a mixed group with some technically inclined friends. A friend with mediocre awareness might start talking about server architecture, which can be fascinating if all people are interested in it, but is intensely boring if you're not technically inclined. In those situations I will cut the conversation as short as possible without even looking to see if everyone's engaged. I can safely make the assumption that they aren't.

If my friend manages to engage me in a technical discussion, I'll keep it as short as possible, and then I'll immediately switch to a topic that will engage the others, even if it will alienate him a bit. Most likely I would turn to a non-engaged person and ask them about a trip they went on or their family or something that they'll love to talk about. That way even if I can't keep everyone engaged in the short term, everyone will have talked about interesting things over the course of the evening.

One particular situation to be aware of is when you are with a friend and their significant other. When you know one person very well and have a lot of inside jokes and common knowledge, many of your usual conversations will alienate everyone else, including significant others. In that situation, I'll almost always engage the significant other quickly. I can assume that my friend will recognize that I'm being considerate towards his girlfriend, and that he'll be glad that I'm engaging her.

If I'm the significant other in the equation, I'm happy to allow the other two to talk as they please, but I'm also inclined to use it as an opportunity to get to know my girlfriend's friends and to take the responsibility of accommodating me off their hands.

Know That You're Probably Wrong All The Time

I consider myself to be an intelligent person, and yet I've been wrong so many times in my life. I was vegan for a while, and now I eat meat. Each time I switched because I believed the other diet to be healthier. So we can be assured that I was wrong at least once between those two decisions. I've been sure of facts, bet my friends, and then lost those bets. I remember being convinced a mechanic was wrong as he diagnosed a boat motor, and then watching as he fixed it in seconds.

It never feels good to be wrong, but I'm glad to have been wrong so many times. For one, it gives me proof that I'm actually learning, and second it has beaten into submission my confidence that I'm always right about everything. And that's made me a better conversationalist.

No one ever thinks that they're wrong in an argument, and yet at least fifty percent of people are (sometimes both can be wrong). If you're hanging out with people of approximately your same intellectual level, your odds of being right are around fifty percent. And if you're only hanging out with people much less intelligent than yourself, you're probably doing yourself a big disservice.

It's fine to have an argument with someone and believe that you're right. Some people really like debating each other, and it can actually bring people closer. But when one or both people refuse to admit the possibility that they could be wrong, the argument can be destructive.

So go in knowing the odds. You're just as likely to be right as wrong. If you realize that you're wrong, don't cling to your old belief to be safe or save face. Give your friend the satisfaction and respect of having convinced you, and he'll be more likely to admit when he's wrong next time.

If you don't do this, and you always believe that you're right and never give an inch of doubt, people won't want to argue with you. They'll avoid any topic that's remotely controversial and you'll find yourself unable to engage in meaningful debate.

Remember that it's not important to be right in the beginning, only in the end. And if your friend gets the satisfaction of teaching you something as you become right, that's a good thing for both of you.

Being Relatable

A friend came to me with a really interesting problem. He has a very exciting life, traveling constantly, going on adventures, and running his own business. Sometimes when he talks to people with dissimilar lives, he finds that he becomes alienated. Is that preventable, or is it just how he's going to have to relate to people with more conventional lives?

The solution is to downplay and be more relatable. People are most comfortable hanging out and talking with people that they can relate to. They can be confident that those people will accept them and be interested in what they have to say. But if you seem like your life is radically different, they can become insecure and either withdraw or try to cut you down to their level.

Try to imagine how the person or group you're interacting with thinks. What motivates them? To what do they ascribe their successes and failures? What is an average day like? What qualities do they respect? What do they like to do?

Once you can conceive of these things, shape your conversation to match. For example, my friend was talking to people who probably rarely travel. They work normal jobs and aren't particularly ambitious or proactive. He should avoid talking about travel at all, or, if the topic comes up in conversation, he should say, "Oh, I was just in Europe. I got a crazy deal on a ticket, so I couldn't pass it up."

There's no way they can interpret that as him thinking he's better than them. They can imagine being lucky and getting a good deal on a trip. They probably won't even ask where in Europe he traveled. It's just too far from their reality to be a relevant detail.

Of course, sometimes you'll meet someone who is genuinely interested in the details and keeps probing. No problem obliging them-- the point is to share the information they'll most relate to, and then to allow them to choose how much of the other information they receive.

For his job, which is self-directed and rather impressive, I'd try to couch it as much as possible as a normal person's job. Instead of listing off all of my sites, blog, an books I've written, I always just say "I'm a writer" in those situations. If people ask for more information, I'm happy to give it to them, but I'm wary of explanations that could be construed as bragging.

A couple years ago some friends and I bought a small island. Most people assume that this means I'm a millionaire, but the truth is that it was cheaper than the median priced home in the US, and we split it ten ways. Even so, you can imagine that telling people about our island can be alienating.

So when I come back from a trip there and someone asks where I'm traveling from, I just say "Nova Scotia". If they ask why, I might say that some friends and I bought some land there. If they ask for the whole story I'll tell them everything.

Of course, If I were talking with someone I perceived to be higher status than me, or just someone else who does cool projects, I would just say that I came back from an island I bought with my friends and wouldn't worry that it would make me unrelatable.

Just because you downplay to people who might be intimidated doesn't mean that you should exaggerate to those on the other end of the spectrum. A little bit of modesty is appreciated by everyone, but exaggeration sours people quickly and makes them assume everything you say might be an exaggeration.

Remember that there's a difference between someone liking you and someone being impressed by you. Impressing can alienate, but you won't run into any problems making people like you.

Smile and be Positive

Everyone has some sort of self-description. Maybe I'm an adventurous traveler and writer, maybe you're a sarcastic musician and comedian. However you define yourself, add "happy and positive" to the beginning of that description, and be that version of yourself.

People will decide how much time to spend with you primarily based on how they feel when they're around you. Your accomplishments are just enough to get people to want to know you. Whether or not they become good friends with you will have a lot more to do with how they feel while hanging out with you.

If you are cheerful and positive, people will enjoy spending time around you. The happy and positive version of you is the best version you have to offer other people.

If someone is happy and in a great mood, your positivity will only make them feel even better. If someone is having a tough time, your positivity might cheer them up, or at least make them forget their problems for the time.

That doesn't mean you have to joke around all the time, be fake, or be rambunctious. You just want to be positive. Smile and look at the bright side. That's all it takes.

Positivity is even more important in groups than it is

one-on-one. Seven happy excited people can have the wind taken out of their sails by one negative person acting alone. If seven people are having a good time and you end that, you're doing a lot of damage to people that you consider friends.

Being Dynamic

I probably shouldn't say this, as it will make just about everyone feel awkward around me, but I'm constantly analyzing people's social skills. When I really like being around someone, I think a lot about why that's so. There are some people whom I can spend weeks with and still be excited about their company. How do they do that?

The real mysteries, though, are the people who I should like spending time with, but just don't. They're good people, don't rub me the wrong way at all, and yet I can take or leave them. As I see who gets invited to what, I often notice that others feel the same way.

What do these people have in common? What can they do to shift the perception others have of them and be in a better position to share their positive aspects?

The best definition, loose as it is, is that these people lack the quality of being dynamic. They're predictable, reserved, and seem to endeavor to minimize their impact on others.

In my definition, I mean a certain type of being predictable. It's good to be predictably timely, cheerful, and any other number of positive attributes. But there's something really magnetic about someone who brings something different to the interaction every time. You don't know what they'll say. Maybe they'll have a really interesting question they're mulling over, maybe a great new story, or maybe some exciting new place they've found. Their positive contribution to the social interaction is unpredictable.

People who are reserved and minimize their impact succeed in leaving everyone unoffended, but people go to social gatherings for a reason, and that reason is not to be unoffended or remain unimpacted.

Think of the ideal person you'd like to meet or hang out with. A dynamic person. He's going to be excited about something, but you don't know what. He won't sit by in the wings, but will be sharing his excitement with everyone. He enriches the environment both through the content of what he shares, and also through the emotion he brings. His cheerfulness and excitement lift everyone's mood. That's addictive. It makes people want to spend time with him.

He's also looking for the same in the people with whom he interacts. He wants to know what they're excited about, and will try to draw it out of them. He's looking for the chance to bring people out of their shells and be impacted by them.

Some suggestions in this book are optional and you can get by with or without them. I try to include ideas that will appeal to both the socially inept who are making big changes, and the socially adept who are fine-tuning their approach. But being dynamic applies to everyone and is essential. If you think there's any chance you're not very dynamic, improving should be a top priority.

Someone who is dynamic is really engaged with life. He's going through life looking for the interesting and exciting. He's engaged with people, too. It's not enough to find these interesting and exciting things for himself, he must share it with the world.

Make it your mission to look at the world as the wonder that it is. Find the humor and awe in everyday situations. Push yourself out of your comfort zone and experience more than you have before. And then share these things with other people and hone in on their reactions. Look for the signs of the pleasure they get from your impact.

Your Value as a Friend

It's nice to think that everyone is equally wonderful and would make a great friend if you just took the time to know them, but that's probably not true. As a simple, non-controversial example, imagine you cloned yourself, and one clone got rid of bad habits. He would be a better friend as a result. Even if two people were equally good at being friends, there's the issue of compatibility.

This all boils down to value. Not your value as a human being, but the value you bring to any individual friendship. And it's all relative-- a hammer has a lot of value if you need to put some nails into boards, but very little if you need to cut a board in half. Don't get too hung up on the connotations of value, just think of it as what you bring to a specific friendship.

To any person, you'll have some level of intrinsic value. These are things that you are. For example, if you live in the same city as someone, that gives you some intrinsic value. All other things being equal, they'd rather befriend someone who lives nearby. Or maybe you're really funny, which makes you fun to be around.

You also bring value to the friendship via action. If you make dinner for your friends, you're adding value to their lives. If you organize an event for your friends, you're also adding value.

Whether you think about these things or not, or whether you're even able to identify them, they're there. When you really like being friends with someone, it's because they're bringing a lot of value to the friendship. When you stop being friends with someone, it's because they weren't bringing enough.

In certain ways, you're also taking value from your friends. When you drink some milk from their fridge, you've taken a little bit of value from them. When you spread bad rumors about them, you're taking a lot of value from them.

In the end it's a subconscious equation that you're calculating, weighing value taken with value given. As a friend, you want to maximize the value that you give to your friends, both things that you are and things that you do.

A good exercise is to think about what it might be like to be your friend. What would that feel like? What would the good parts of that friendship be? What would the bad parts be? What could you do to make that experience better for the other person?

It's interesting to think about, because some of your positive attributes translate to lots of value, and others into not so much. If you're neat and tidy, that's great for you, but not particularly amazing for your friends. If you're very empathetic, that could bring a lot of value to your friends.

Think also about the things you can do for your

friends and how those things would affect them. How would your friends feel if you make dinner for them once a week? How about if you organized a hike for them?

Friendship is Based on Shared Experiences, Not Time

I have a friend named Derek who has excellent social skills and is particularly good at crossing the line and making himself vulnerable. We met in person once or twice, talked on the phone a bunch of times, and sent a handful of emails back and forth. During one of our phone calls, we were talking about the pros and cons of traveling and making friends; how you get to spend good quality time with people, but that having so many balls in the air means that you may not get to spend all that much time with any given person.

He said that he thought that people overrated time spent together. For example, he said, we're really good friends even though we've only hung out in person a couple of times.

I'd never thought about that, but the more I did, the more it made sense. There were some friends I'd had for years with whom I wouldn't share personal problems and whose company I wouldn't go out of my way to share. On the other hand, my friend who brought this up was someone with whom I would readily share personal problems. And if he were in a tight spot and needed someone to help him, I'd be there to do it.

I thought a lot about why this was so. How could I be better friends with someone I'd known for a short period of time than someone I'd known for years?

It occurred to me that friendships are mostly based on shared experiences and the realizations and consequences of those experiences. But the trick is that those shared experiences don't have to be synchronous. If two people do similar things in their childhoods, they'll probably have a lot of common values and experiences to talk about. If not, they have a lot of ground to cover. They can still become best friends, but it might take a bit longer.

Derek and I were both a little bit rebellious towards authority, had both stumbled upon programming early, and had done similar types of travel. We'd both become minimalists and valued similar things.

These are the sorts of friends where you both seem to understand each other immediately. It's very easy to rapidly become friends with someone when you have a lot of similar experiences in your pasts.

If you don't have those similar experiences, then you'll probably have to create them. The catch is that you can't just do the same thing together all the time. That's just one shared experience, repeated indefinitely. That's why there are some acquaintances that never become friends, no matter how much time you spend with them. You don't have those shared common experiences, and you aren't really creating them either.

Introductions

Introductions are the fundamental currency of expansive social skills; that is, building your friend group or making friends in different circles. The power of this particular currency, however, is that rather than lose it, you earn more by spending it wisely. Receiving introductions is fantastic, but giving them out is even better.

One of your top social priorities should be helping others meet their future best friends. Among your first thoughts upon getting to know someone should be: who do I know who would love this person? Who of the people I know would they love?

By making an introduction, you manifest a huge benefit for three people out of thin air. The two people introduced get to know someone great, and you get the credit for it. If someone knows that you're thinking about them and trying to introduce them to great people, chances are they're going to start thinking about you and return the favor. And one introduction creates two people doing that.

The most important thing to realize about introductions is that the most valuable role you can play isn't to be a friend provider, but to be a friend filter. The benefit you're offering isn't to put someone in front of them, but rather to put your stamp of approval on that person.

I have an incredible group of friends. Every day I

think about how fortunate I am to have such kind and smart people as fixtures in my life. The problem, though, is that I also stay busy with work, so my social time is limited. For me to take time away from the pool of time I could spend with my amazing friends, it probably has to come through an introduction. Having a great social circle demotivates me from meeting up with unknown people who want to meet with me.

But if one of my friends who knows me well, knows my values, and knows how busy I am suggests that I meet someone, I often make the time. We don't click one hundred percent of the time, but some of my very best friends have been made this way. As I write this, a friend I met through a filtered introduction is sitting a few feet away, working on his own project.

By introducing two people, you also become a part of their relationship. The three of you will do things together, and they'll talk positively about you when you're not there. So if there's someone you're working on building a friendship with, making an introduction can help solidify the friendship.

So besides the literally life-changing amount of good a well thought out introduction can do for the people being introduced, it will also be a really positive thing for you. Don't be selfish with your friends-- introduce them and share them with other great people you know.

Think about what it would take for you to introduce

someone to a new friend. Not a best friend with whom you have a really solid lifelong friendship, but someone you really like and are building a new friendship with. Besides thinking that the two people would be a good fit, you would also have to consider how the new friend will react if they don't get along.

There are two ways in which people don't get along. Sometimes they will like each other, but just not be interested in being friends. This happens all the time and is still a net positive. Let's say that you think there's a chance they'll become good friends, and a fifty percent chance they'll have a nice tea together, but won't ever want to meet up again. Even if the latter happens, both are thankful that you thought of them, and think just as highly of you as before.

On the other hand, there are situations where people meet and they strongly dislike each other. They don't respect each other or they offend each other. Maybe your new friend is a really solid stable person and the person you're considering introducing is a loose cannon. He's an artist who is fascinating and smart, but he's also moody and sometimes does things for shock value and offends people. Even if you think there's a ninety percent chance the two will get along, you'll be hesitant to introduce them, and may decide not to do so. You'd be justified in making that decision, as the introduction could damage your new friendship and cause him to misjudge you.

The important takeaway from this is to realize that you cannot afford to be that liability. Some of your best friendships will probably come through introductions, and being a loose cannon will shut down your opportunities to meet people through friends.

For this reason, your primary goal when being introduced is to make your friend look really good. It's not to make yourself look good, it's to make your friend look good.

First of all, it's just the right thing to do. Your friend put his reputation on the line a little bit by vouching for you, whether or not you make a new friend. You want that to pay off for him every time, so you make him look good. You talk about what a great friend he is, share good stories about him, and constantly remember that your behavior will reflect on him whether you intend for it to or not.

Let's say that I was friends with the Queen of England (I'm not). I would never have to worry about her meeting anyone I introduced her to. There's just a zero percent chance she's going to make a bad impression on someone. So if she asked to meet anyone I know, I would immediately make it happen. The person meeting her would have a great experience, so she would look good, but it would earn points for me, too.

You want to be the Queen of England. You want to be the person who any of your friends can introduce to anyone they know and be sure that it will make them look good. Besides getting more high-quality introductions, this also ensures that your friends can give you a really positive introduction. They can say great things about you and don't have to hedge it. If you might be a liability, they talk you up a lot, and you end up offending them, all of a sudden your introducing friend looks really bad. If they're worried that's the case, you get an introduction like, "Alice is a great person, but once in a while she..."

If you don't get a lot of introductions or if you ask for them and they somehow don't end up happening, you are probably more of a liability than you realize. Work on the other stuff in this book and think critically about what would stop people from introducing you. The benefits are worth the discomfort of discovering some personal flaws that need work.

We're all connected by approximately six degrees of separation. Meaning that I know someone who knows someone who knows someone who knows someone who knows someone who knows you. Since we speak the same language and are both interested in social skills, it's probably more like two or three. The same goes for anyone you want to meet. You're probably only three or four degrees away. The way you hop those degrees is by getting into the introductions game, making them for your friends and making sure you're the type of person whom people would want to introduce.

Look for Side Doors

One of the great things about making friends in school is that pretty much everyone is accessible and has a lot of time to socialize. In the real world, though, that becomes less true, especially as some people become more sought after due to popularity or time constraints.

When someone becomes even moderately well-known, especially in a public forum like the internet, the requests for his time will quickly outpace the number of hours in the day. Declining invitations and ignoring emails becomes a necessity.

As this happens, the requests also become more homogeneous. The email starts out with a compliment and statement on how much the recipient is respected, and then quickly transitions into a request to meet up for coffee. "Hey, I love your books and have read all of them. I'm coming to your city next month and was hoping we could get coffee."

This is an attempt to get through a front door that's mobbed with people, and quite possibly locked to keep the masses out. The success rate is somewhere near zero.

I'm not particularly famous, but enough people read my blog and books that I have to lock my front door. I used to meet up with people, then I moved to just declining politely most of the time, and now I just ignore the emails, because answering them, and the ensuing follow-ups, would take up too much time.

One day I got an email from a long-time reader, asking if I wanted photography lessons. He was friends with a famous photographer, and offered to fly to my city with him and have him teach me some things about shooting.

It sounds like a bribe, and sort of is, but mostly it's a side door. His approach was so different than everyone else's that I didn't have a blanket policy that covered it. I had to evaluate the invitation individually, and ended up accepting.

Another time a woman emailed me saying that I was her husband's favorite blogger, and she wanted to fly him to my city under the guise of a romantic weekend away, and then have me show up for tea as a surprise. The idea was so fun that I happily said yes.

I've done the same thing to meet people. In a previous life I was one of the pickup artists written about in the book, The Game. When I moved to San Francisco and wanted to meet entrepreneurs, most of them wouldn't have wanted to meet just another guy starting just another startup. But I had skills that were in short supply in those circles, and they opened a lot of doors. Side doors.

When contacting someone who might not reply to you because he's too busy, or when trying to get him to hang out with you for the first time, think about what sorts of requests he gets a lot of, and which he gets none of. What can you do or say that will get his attention? Sharing unique skills you have is a reliable standard, but you can also think about events you can invite the person to, people you can introduce him to, or experiences you can create for him.

You could think of this as bribing people for their time, which feels a bit unpalatable. But the best and most accurate way to think about it is as a realist: many of the people you may want to meet are busy and get so many requests to meet that they must say no. Trying to go through the front door won't work, so if you really want to get to know them, you've got to find a side door.

Host a Weekly Event

My friend Nick is probably the most socially skilled person I know, especially in terms of building and managing large groups of friends. I've been inspired by many of the things he does, maybe none as much as the weekly events he hosts.

Nick has an apartment in New York. It's small and five stories up, but it's in a prime location that makes it easy for anyone in the city to access. Every week he has an extremely casual dinner party. He orders some Thai takeout, invites a bunch of people over, and they sit around his apartment talking and eating Thai food.

The great thing about the weekly event isn't that you get to have a fun time with your friends, but rather that you create a very convenient track for someone to become your friend.

When you first meet someone and want to become better friends, one of you has to take the initiative and invite the other to do something. Since you're going to be taking responsibility for the friendships in your life, that person will be you. But inviting someone to a one-on-one thing can sometimes be awkward. If the person is of the opposite sex, it could be construed as a date even if it's not. And even inviting someone of the same sex to an event can feel a little weird. Going from stranger to one-on-one can be a big jump.

But it's very easy to invite someone to come join you and your friends for food next Sunday. As Nick meets interesting people throughout the week, he invites them to come to dinner at his place. It's an easy invitation to say yes to, and most do. It seems like every time I go, there are a few regulars and a bunch of people I've never met before.

You can also make people into regulars and rapidly accelerate how quickly you become friends. I happened to invite a few people to have dinner with one of my best friends and me. I wanted to become better friends with them, so I just kept inviting them every week. Now they're some of my closest friends and the weekly dinner tradition continues even when I'm out of town traveling.

Very often in the early stages of friendships, you don't know the person well enough to go through the hassle of negotiating a time and place to meet. You wouldn't mind making the time, but you're both busy, so it just doesn't happen regularly. Sometimes you go months without seeing each other. But a standing weekly event is very easy to do, and requires no commitment. If they're free they come, otherwise they don't.

I'd recommend starting with a very simple weekly event. Pick an off night like Sunday, and just agree to have dinner at the same place every week. It's easy to remember, doesn't cost you anything more than your dinner, and the focus is on people and conversation. Find a core group of friends that will go with you every week, maybe people you're hoping to get to know better, and then all of you can invite people you meet to the dinner. Now you have an easy way to begin new friendships.

Travel is a Friendship Shortcut

It all started by accident. I booked an extraordinarily cheap trip to Japan and excitedly tweeted about it. A reader whom I'd met once, and liked, booked similar dates with at least a week of overlap. As I'm really familiar with Japan, I offered to show him around by train.

The flight wasn't for another nine months, so as the weeks went on I told more and more friends about the trip. All of them had heard me talk about Japan throughout the years, so many were interested in coming along. Before I knew it, I had a group of ten people, ranging from really close friends to people I'd never actually met in person.

I'm now close friends with everyone I invited on that trip. Some of them became close friends with each other, too. As I write this, I'm on another trip with the guy I'd never met, and I've actually bought property with the reader who was the first to join the trip.

The quantity and depths of friendships created during that single week is amazing. In an average week, I make zero new friendships and deepen existing ones slightly. That one week significantly deepened several friendships and created at least two new ones.

This was such a fantastic use of time that the trip has become an annual tradition and has been supplemented with twice-annual transoceanic group cruises. Each of these has spawned and deepened friendships, both for me and the others on the trips.

Why does this work? I think there are a lot of reasons, but two major ones.

First, you rack up a huge number of shared experiences in a very short amount of time. On the first cruise to Japan, we ran to catch trains, climbed up boulders on the top of a mountain, visited a tea farm, hiked between some famous temples, sang karaoke, and ate at a robotic sushi restaurant. That's a lot of positive memories to share. It's also a slightly different view of the world that we all got to see at the same time. None of us were completely transformed by the trip, but each of our lives was slightly altered as a result. That's something we have in common.

Second, some of the most interesting people you'll meet are also the busiest. You don't become interesting by being idle. Often the only way you're actually going to get a chance to become good friends with interesting people is to separate them from their normal life. This is one reason I particularly like cruises. Being on a cruise is such a bizarre and foreign experience, situated way out in the middle of the ocean, that it may as well be another world. Plenty of time to sit down and really get to know someone.

Travel doesn't have to be exotic or faraway to be a great binder, though. My friend Olivia has an annual event where she rents a house out in a redwood forest. She invites a ton of friends who each split the cost, so it's not a huge burden on her. We have nice long meals that we take turns cooking, hikes through the woods, and plenty of time to just sit around and chat or play games. Even though it's only an hour away from where most of us live, it's still a big enough shift to have the exact same effect as the trips to Japan.

Traveling is a great way to make yourself more interesting, if you feel like being interesting is something you need to work on. It puts you in enough unusual situations that you build a bank of stories and experiences, and it gives you perspective you wouldn't have otherwise gotten. Couple that with trips with your friends, new and old, and it becomes an extremely valuable social activity.

Focus On Important Friendships

For most of my life, deciding how to spend my time wasn't much of a struggle. I had a few close friends, wasn't outgoing enough to make more, and had a lot of free time. So if someone wanted to hang out, I'd probably be able to go join them without much thought. But then, a few years ago, that changed.

I had become consumed with my work. I'd stay home all day, sitting in front of the computer, chipping away at the work that lay before me. I loved being so productive, but all of a sudden I didn't have very much social time. I struggled to see all of my friends, and realized that I didn't actually have the time to spend enough quality time with them.

So I decided that I would stop hanging out with everyone except for my closest friends and new friends that I was really interested in becoming better friends with. I started saying no to most social invitations, including those with good friends where I felt it wouldn't be quality time. So I'd go have tea with a good friend, but wouldn't go to a birthday party of a friend's friend.

I never really thought about what the effects of this would be. It wasn't a calculated choice-- it was just a quick reaction to feeling like I was neglecting my best friends.

What happened, though, was really remarkable. I didn't miss any of the social events I was now skipping. I'd feel a slight fear of missing out when I declined, but then when it was over, I was always really happy with how I used my time instead. But I expected that.

The surprise was what happened with existing friendships. By focusing all of my social time on my favorite people, my relationships with them improved. And the new friends who I kept seeing became better and better friends quickly.

Focus is such a powerful tool in learning and work, but we underestimate its benefit socially. By focusing my limited time on the people that matter most to me, those friendships become and stay very strong. And my social time is better than ever, because all of it is with my favorite people or new people I'm excited to get to know.

It can be scary and counterintuitive, when trying to improve your social skills, to say no to invitations or to trim down your roster of friends, but the focus makes it worth it. The goal isn't to have a million friends, it's to have a close group of amazing friends.

Different Types of Friendships

While it's always a good thing to have a local friend group that you cultivate and build, that doesn't mean that that's the only type of friendship worth having or putting effort into. In particular, you can have very deep and satisfying friendships even if you don't see the other person very often. You'd prefer to have the best people live right near you and be able to hang out in person whenever you're available, but that's not always possible. The "right person" part is the important part, though, and it's worth investing in people even if the logistics aren't great.

For example, I have some friends in Austin who I love to death but only get to see once or twice per year. We don't talk much on the phone or online when I'm not there, but as soon as I land in Austin, it's like I never left. Sure, I'd rather that they live near me and travel with me a lot, but even though they don't, they're still close and valued friends.

I have a lot of friends who travel so much that we're always in flux. They'll come visit Las Vegas, but I won't be home, and then I'll be in New York, and they're off traveling somewhere else. But every year or so we happen to be in some random country at the same time, and we get to reconnect.

Some friendships will be based on lots of time together, others on lots of conversations on the phone, and some just based on a few intense episodes together over the years.

And you never know when people, including yourself, will move. Life is unpredictable for all of us. So even if you meet someone while traveling and don't know if or when you'll ever see them again, it's worth pursuing the friendship. Do that enough times and you'll have the odds on your side for serendipitously reconnecting with them in the future.

On Not Being Intimidated

Sometimes you'll meet someone, or be trying to meet someone, who is intimidating. They seem so accomplished and funny and smart that you begin to question whether what you have to offer stacks up at all with what they have to offer.

There are two common approaches to this problem, neither of which works very well.

The first is to come in low. You act like a fan, ask a ton of questions to get a dialogue going, and then wait for an invitation of some sort. By doing this, you communicate low value and push the other person away. He'll be polite to you, but will almost immediately rule out friendship. Not feeling like you have enough to offer becomes a self-fulfilling prophecy.

The second way is to come in high. You don't acknowledge the other person's accomplishments and you compensate for your perceived lack of status by trying to impress. This always rings hollow, makes you seem inauthentic, and will also push the other person away.

So what can you do?

The first thing to realize is that you just have to bring one thing, plus good social skills, to the table for someone to be interested in being your friend. Good social skills ensure that you don't impose on the other person, and one major positive source of value is enough to make someone want to be your friend. Even the most sought after people like to have someone around who's funny, or tells good stories, or organizes cool events.

And no one is as good as their image suggests. Everyone has their weaknesses and insecurities. So even if someone seems like they're perfect, you can safely assume that they're not. They're probably an impressive person with a lot going for them, but no one is better than you in every way. You always have something to offer.

Treat everyone as an equal, not because they are, but because they can be. People will often take on roles foisted upon them in social situations, and everyone is used to having peers around. If you act like a peer, you will usually be treated like one.

In a situation where the other person is probably very selective in whom they hang out with, usually because of time constraints, think about what it is you have to offer that will appeal to them, and convey it as early as possible. That means that instead of allowing them to talk, if they prefer to talk than to listen, you make an effort to tell your stories to establish what makes you unique.

If they're in a setting where other people are coming in low and high, versus a setting amongst their established peers, you should also be inclined to joke around more. This will allow you to stand out even more, since others will be too intimidated to joke around. Besides demonstrating intelligence, joking around also demonstrates comfort, something that is possibly in short supply in that situation.

Remember Names

My friend Todd used to have a small text file on his phone. Every time he met anyone, and I mean anyone, he would write down their name and a few little details about them. So if he checked out at the supermarket and exchanged more than a "Hello, plastic please...", he'd write down the cashier's name and a couple things about her that got brought up.

Most of the time he'd never run into that person again, and he'd just have another name in his file. But every time he would go into a store or a party, he'd look at his list and quickly refresh his memory on people's names. Over time he'd have more hits, and would be able to greet people by name and maybe ask them about something they'd mentioned the time before.

I'm not sure there was a more liked person in all of Austin, Texas. Every restaurant we'd go to, he'd be saying hi to people by name, they'd remember his name, and just be so happy to see him. Some of those people ended up becoming his friends, too.

It's sort of silly, when you think about it. Your name is the least interesting part of who you are, and yet it's disproportionately flattering when someone remembers it. So, even if it seems a little bit trivial, the act of remembering people's names is important.

The problem is that when you first meet someone, you are being bombarded by interesting information about them. You are making inferences from their appearance, listening to what they have to say, sizing them up, and trying to understand the interpersonal dynamics at play. With all of that going on, you hear their name and then immediately forget it.

There are memory tricks to remember names, but there's also a simpler solution. A minute or two into the conversation, just ask for their name again. No one is ever offended, because most people are bad at remembering names, and those that aren't know how rare a skill they have. In fact, most people are a little bit flattered-- you're indicating that they've reached a threshold of importance to you where you need to know their name.

Most of the time you'll then remember their name forever. Once you have the context of knowing them a little bit as a person, their name will be a lot stickier and remembering it will no longer be a struggle. You can also use Todd's trick and just write it down with a little bit of background information every time. It's a minor hassle that pays large dividends.

Start With Your Family

Family is really important to my mother. It's important to everyone in my family, but I get the impression it's not just her number one priority in life, but the one that she thinks about most of the time. I remember once we were talking about my siblings, and she made an offhand comment that they were potentially the most important relationships in my life. After all, they were the people I'd know for the longest and have the most context with.

She was right, and it really made me think differently about my siblings. We were always close and got along really well, but I decided to be a little bit more proactive about seeing them and spending time with them.

I spend a lot of time with my family, both immediate and extended. I reflect a lot on our relationships, and I'm always struck by the bond we have. Some of us would be friends if we weren't related, some of us would probably be too different, but our common familial bond covers a lot of that distance.

It's a shortcut. Creating a close relationship with a family member takes a fraction of the effort it would take to create a relationship with an acquaintance. You're already on the same team, and there are a lot of forces working in unison to build a friendship between the two of you.

And familial relationships can be some of the most

rewarding. The benefit I've received over the years from my siblings, parents, aunts and uncles, cousins, and grandparents is huge. Even more than friends, they give a sense of belonging and unconditional love.

So it's easiest to create friendships with family members, and often more rewarding than other types of friendships. If you have trouble making friends or are looking for a comfortable place to practice your social skills, start with your family. They're rooting for you already, and will be a part of your life as long as anyone will be.

Focus on Friends, Eliminate Acquaintances

To simplify, let's say that there are three groups into which you could slot people you know. On the outside are acquaintances, next are friends, and in the center are close friends.

Acquaintances could be defined as people you'd only hang out with one-on-one if it were extremely convenient. Most of your interactions are probably in group settings, you only end up having a one-on-one conversation by accident, and you'd never invite the other to something alone.

Friends are people you hang out with when convenient, maybe through shared interests. You don't connect on a deep emotional level, but maybe you really enjoy playing tennis together. You'll have meals together sometimes, but you wouldn't change your plans for them.

Close friends are the people you love. They're the people for whom you'd act against your best interests if the benefit to them was significant. They're the people whose success feels almost as good as your own, and with whom you can spend almost any length of time.

The value you exchange with an acquaintance is minimal. A trifle of entertainment, a conversational partner when you're desperate for one, maybe a positive memory or two. Your limited power to benefit them is on par with their limited power to benefit you.

On the other end of the scale are close friends. The value exchanged between two close friends is enormous. In fact, many studies show that people with more close ties to others live longer. There are a few major factors that will define who you are, and close friendships are one of the big ones.

The thing that people don't often think about, though, is that an hour spent with acquaintances costs the same as an hour spent with good friends. Sixty minutes either way, one hour with tremendous power behind it, and the other promising nothing beyond the superficial.

When examined through this lens, spending time with acquaintances is often a poor use of time. The alternative is simply too positive to ignore. That's not to say that you can't make the best of that time and help others have a good time, just that there's a high cost to it.

Just as every tree begins as a seed, every close friendship begins as an acquaintance. Spending time with acquaintances who might become close friends someday is a very good use of time. The trap that people fall into is when they hang out with acquaintances and friends with whom they'll never have a deeper relationship. Sometimes they do it out of loneliness, other times for superficial fun. Those are trade-offs that can be made, but it's important to know the cost.

Think very carefully about how you spend your social time. I'd say that one of the biggest indicators into how good someone's friend group is going to be in a few years is how high of a percentage of that time is spent with either close friends or people with clear potential to become close friends.

When you have friends or acquaintances with whom you don't want a closer friendship, or who don't want a closer friendship with you, it's best to cease all effort to spend time with them. That doesn't mean not to be friendly and kind to them, just to make the best use of your time as well as theirs.

Treat Everyone Well

When I speak about cutting out acquaintances and being protective about how you spend your social time, it can come across as being cold and hostile. That's not the intention, though, and it's not how it translates in real life. As an inviolable rule, I believe in treating everyone well.

You have incomplete control over how you spend your time. You can try to maximize the time spent with good friends and people moving towards becoming good friends, but sometimes you'll be at a party with a different crowd than you'd choose, or you'll be in a line in the airport with people you didn't choose at all.

You completely control how you treat other people, unlike how you control your time. In any given situation, you have complete agency to be friendly or unfriendly, cold or warm.

When you decide to treat someone well, you are creating goodwill and positive emotions out of nothing. Sometimes the effects of your manner will be small, but other times they'll have a huge impact on another person. You just never know, and there's a lot of variance.

While you may have a good idea how a close friend is feeling, you'll generally have less of an idea how an acquaintance or stranger feels. They could be feeling great, and you being a little bit short could throw them into a bad mood. Or maybe they're already in a bad mood and you being unnecessarily kind to them helps cheer them up.

You also benefit from treating people well. Friendships start in unexpected places, and treating someone well who gave you a bad first impression could lead to you getting to knowing them better and changing your opinion of them. Being kind to people feels good to you and them.

Treating people well is a no-brainer. It takes very little effort, benefits everyone, and could lead to new friendships. The reasons for not doing it, like generating a feeling of superiority or not wanting to waste a few seconds, don't hold up against the benefits. Be selective about in whom you invest time and become friends with, but treat everyone else like friends as much as possible.

Choose Friends Because You Love Them

I got an introduction to a guy who was really big in the tech industry, the industry I was in at the time. We chatted for a while, and then hung out a few times after that. We always had a good time joking around and talking about tech.

After hanging out a few times, I could tell that we were just never going to become close friends. Lots of mutual respect, but just different priorities, interests, and lifestyles. So I stopped making an effort to hang out, and we haven't seen each other since.

A huge part of me wanted to continue to be friends with him, just because of who he was. I felt really cool being associated with him, and I couldn't help but think that my startup might have an advantage if I just forced a friendship.

But it didn't feel like a very genuine thing to do, especially when I realized that I probably wouldn't have made an effort to be friends with him if he wasn't who he was.

In the time I would have spent with him, and other superficial friendships, I met new people who I really connected with. Having such good friendships, I'm glad I realized the difference between making friends and making connections.

It's great when you meet someone who is interesting and accomplished and impressive. If you click, and become good friends with them, that's a good thing for both people. But when you try to force a friendship because you want something from them, you're building a house on a rocky foundation. You may derive some benefit from the association, but it's dishonest and it takes time and focus away from real friendships you could create.

Choose friends not because of what they can do for you, but because you love who they are.

Know What You're Looking For

Most people passively wait for friendships to spontaneously sprout, even though being proactive about the process is a lot more effective. Even when you're actively engaging with the process, though, it takes time and effort. Anything you can do to make the process efficient will improve your results.

One such thing is knowing what it is you like in a friend. Even if you have a broad range of friends, there are probably a few key attributes that they share. Once you know those attributes, you can make it a priority to look for them in new people you meet, and then follow up with the people who have them.

I have a wide range of friends. Some travel all the time, some stay in one place. A bunch are in tech, but one is an acupuncturist, one is a cage fighter, and another makes pies. Some are republican, some are democrat. They live in all different places in the world.

One day I challenged myself to figure out what it was that I liked in common in all my friends. Although they were different in a lot of ways, it felt as though there was some intangible similarity shared by all of them. After a lot of thinking, I realized that nearly every one was someone who was smart, ambitious, and extremely kind.

Those sound like generic positive attributes, but a lot of the most ambitious people aren't all that kind.

Maybe they're nice, but, to me at least, being kind means something more significant.

Knowing what my friends had in common turned out to be more practical knowledge than I had expected. Having discovered what my filter was, I was constantly evaluating people to determine how kind, smart, and ambitious they were. Instead of finding these things out in a roundabout fashion over a few hours, I'd focus early on those few attributes.

It also made it easier for me to spend my time with people. When deciding between work or hanging out with a new acquaintance, I'd err strongly on the side of hanging out with them if they were smart, ambitious, and kind.

If you know what you're looking for, you can also make structural changes to your life. What city has those sorts of people? A friend of mine was having trouble making really good friends in LA, but when we figured out what her favorite people had in common, I told her that she had to move to San Francisco. It was where "her people" are. She moved and is now part of an amazing friend group and is happier than she's been in years.

You can also think about what a person who matches your description would want in a friend. Are you that person? If not, maybe that's a hint that you need to shift your direction a little bit. For example, I'm trying to focus on being more kind, because kind people like other kind people.

And you can think about where in your city your type of people hang out. Everywhere will have a range of people, but I think some fair general statements can be made on the people who hang out in coffee shops, nightclubs, bookstores, and parks.

It's a fun exercise, thinking about what your favorite people have in common. If you feel like you don't mesh well with your current friends, think about what the people whom you admire most and would like to be friends with have in common. Once you know, filter new acquaintances through those criteria and adjust your effort accordingly.

Do What You Say, Be Honest, Be On Time

Part of building your social circle is finding ways to stand out in positive ways. People who don't get noticed are never disliked or hated, but they also aren't sought out. Not standing out also makes receiving introductions less likely. An introducer should be able to say something like, "You've got to meet Mary. She's really insightful and always asks questions that lead to interesting conversations."

One easy way too stand out is to find positive attributes that most people don't have and then build them. These get noticed and appreciated, and one way to measure the strength of a friend group is the breadth of positive attributes contained within it. Three undervalued positive attributes are doing what you say, being honest, and being on time. There are many others, but these are three that you can begin immediately and will never go unnoticed.

Doing What You Say

Have you ever met up with someone and, during the course of a long conversation, come up with a few things that you were going to follow up on? Maybe you were going to give him a book recommendation, he was going to send you a link to something, and you were going to put him in touch with someone. And then it just doesn't happen. You sort of knew it wouldn't happen in the moment, but you never get an email from him and you keep putting off your follow-ups until they're so embarrassingly late that you decide to bail on them.

You won't make enemies doing that, but it's a huge opportunity to pass up. Almost no one actually expects that people will follow up without prompting, so if you're the one person who does, you'll stand out in people's minds forever. Every time someone actually follows through, I remember it for a really long time.

Be extremely vigilant about when you tell someone that you're going to do something. Make it a personal goal to follow up as soon as possible and to never fail to do it. It's best to write it down on your phone when you make the promise, but if you don't do that, ask yourself after every social interaction whether you made any commitments that need to be acted upon.

Be Really Honest

You don't have to be a liar to not be honest all of the time. Most people have good intentions and want to positively affect other people, but that very desire prevents them from being honest. They tell someone that their new business idea is great when it's actually a disaster waiting to happen, they say that they like something to fit in, or they hold back an opinion to avoid ruffling feathers.

I won't argue that there isn't a time and place for each of these things, but most people are dishonest in these ways far more often than is appropriate.

Honesty is refreshing. Most people can handle it and appreciate it when it comes, but the majority only receive it from their closest friends.

If you can be honest early in a friendship, you're bringing a lot of value. Maybe that guy needs to hear that his business idea is bad, and your telling him so will help him refine it into something better or use his time doing something more likely to succeed. Maybe by being the brave one to say that you don't want to do something, you're giving a voice to shy people in the group who don't mind agreeing with you, but didn't want the spotlight on them for dissenting. And maybe bringing up an unpopular opinion will spark an interesting debate, rather than more talk about the weather.

If you are consistently honest, even at the risk of inviting disagreement, your friends can trust everything you say, including the good things. Compliments mean more from people who don't give them out unless they're actually true.

Honesty takes bravery because it makes you vulnerable to criticism from others. White lies and careful omissions are a shield. But people respect and want to be friends with honest and brave people.

Being On Time

A special case of doing what you say is being on time. Most people aren't usually grossly late to appointments, but five or fifteen minutes late here and there is often the default. Although you can get away with this, you will be noticed and appreciated if you switch to always being on time.

Being on time also shows a tremendous amount of respect, especially in groups. It says that my convenience isn't more important than minutes of your day. If I'm ten minutes late to a group event that has six other people, I've gained ten minutes of time at the cost of an hour for my friends. I wouldn't take sixty dollars from my friends to make ten dollars, so why would I do it with minutes?

A side benefit of always being on time is that it can influence everyone else to be prompt as well. When they know that you'll definitely be waiting if they show up late, it means more to them and they make the effort to be on time. One of my friends told me that whenever I'm in town, everyone is a lot more prompt because they know that I'm also prompt. So it benefits everyone-- my friends have less wasted time, as do I.

Goals of a Friend Group

Before we delve into the mechanics of building a friend group, it's important to understand what the purpose of this group is. After all, it would be difficult to build a machine without having a clear idea of what the machine was supposed to do once completed.

The primary goal of a friend group is to create a group of people, all of whose lives are disproportionately improved by being a part of the group. If someone can put X units of effort into the group and only gets X units of enjoyment back out, he's not really benefiting from the friend group.

Too often people think about what people can do for them, but they don't think about the balancing part of that formula. They think about how much fun they'd have if they were part of a circle, not the fun they could bring to that circle. But that group won't be sustainable, or at least you won't remain a part of it, unless everyone benefits significantly.

A friend group should be a group of people who will be honest with each other when they need it. If you're dating someone who isn't a good match for you, it's your friend group who should be the ones to do the difficult job of letting you know it's time to look for someone else.

A friend group should be a default group of people to do activities with. If you find an event or class that you want to go to, you should have a reasonable expectation of finding someone within your group to do those things with.

A friend group should be an emotional support system. While effort should be made to keep the atmosphere of the group fun and positive, it's inevitable that each member will go through peaks and valleys throughout their life. Your closest friends are the ones who you should rely on for support in those times.

A friend group should be small enough that each person can have a relationship with every other one. It's fun to be part of a larger social circle, but the group of friends that you work towards building should be small enough that each member can have a meaningful relationship with every other member on an individual basis. Not every pair will be good enough friends to seek out the other's company individually, but many will. Relationships grow differently one-on-one, and having a lot of one-on-one relationships bloom under the umbrella of your friend group makes it much stronger.

A friend group should be able to provide perspective and advice to each other. The best advice comes from two sources: people who know the subject really well and people who know you really well. Ideally you'd have both in one person, but if you don't, a varied group of people who know you well enough to satisfy the latter can be very powerful. Coupled with the honesty mentioned above, your friend group will end up shaping the course of your life.

To build a friend group with these specific components is to build an extremely valuable asset for yourself and for your friends. It can be composed of friends you already have, all new people, or a mix of both.

As time goes on, relationships deepen and people get to know each other better, the friend group becomes even more valuable for everyone involved. If you don't already have a friend group that you love, building one may be the best possible use of your time. The approach I prescribe takes a lot of effort and requires you to assume much of the responsibility, but that's because it's worth it to expend those resources to build something so great.

Being a Leader of Friends

Being a leader isn't a title or something to brag about, it's about serving your friends. Within your friend group, one or more people will have to take leadership roles. You should make the effort to be one of the leaders, because it allows you to bring more value to your group. If there are other leaders, you work in harmony with them, never struggling for power, which causes damage to the group. Leaders of friend groups aren't voted in, they just take power and use it benevolently.

A leader has one main function: to further the interests of the group.

Furthering the interests of the group comes in many flavors. The basic building block of furthering interests is creating opportunities for the group to spend time together and to bond. That could be inviting everyone to play boardgames at your house, planning parties, setting up a weekly tradition, organizing trips, or anything else that brings people together.

You can also bring new interests to the group. I've gotten a bunch of people in my group interested in MMA fighting and the party game, Werewolf. Another friend of mine is really into tea and has converted a bunch of us into tea fanatics. One person can do the exploratory work, find something that would be interesting to everyone, and then teach them about it easily because he knows everyone well.

A friend-of-a-friend of mine bought a bunch of land in upstate New York and built his own version of a summer camp. His friends help him build and maintain it, and now his whole group of friends has a great retreat that they can use. I got to go there for New Years one year and was really in awe of how much he had furthered the interests of his friends by creating such a place.

There are a million different things that you can do for your friends. The general formula is to find something that will multiply your own efforts to benefit all of your friends. This is also why fighting for leadership in a group is counterproductive. Having multiple leaders all working to further the interests of the group benefits everybody.

Create Events

Every event that you and your friends do as a group, on average, will bring you closer together. Whether it's a trip, dinner together, a weekly get-together, or a hike through the woods, each event is like making a deposit in your friend group bank. In any given group, everyone will be willing to go to these events, but only one or a few people are likely to be the driving force making them happen.

You should become one of those people. Your overriding thought in any friend group that you're in should be to ask yourself what you can do to be of service to these people. Anything you do for the group makes the group stronger, and makes it better for everyone, including yourself. It's always worth the time to create the events, because that ensures that they happen.

Don't stress too much about what the events are. They don't need to be run perfectly, or even go all that well. The role of the person setting up the events is to be the spark that sets people in motion. You'll forget what you ate or where you walked, but you'll remember the conversations that took place and the bonds that deepened.

Every group will have people who rely on others to set up activities for the group, and the group can sustain some number of those people without any problems. But since you've decided to be proactive and take responsibility for your social life, you should

do the same for the events that your group goes to.
And if you're more reserved, maybe your action will
push your reserved friends to take a more active role
in the group as well.

This is doubly true if you feel like you don't get
invited to as many things as other people you know.
If you become the one doing the inviting, you induce
others to reciprocate, and you make it obvious that
you're interested in socializing with the group.

Be a Better Friend Than You Have to Be

If there's one area in social skills that is notoriously difficult, it's building an accurate level of self-awareness. Part of what makes it difficult is that you can never be self-aware enough to truly know how self-aware you are. In an ideal situation, you'd be able to gauge the reactions to everything you do, and you'd know both what your strengths and weaknesses are, and the magnitude of each. In reality, even with practice, you'll have only a fuzzy concept of each.

The problem is that your weaknesses will be far more difficult to discover than your strengths. No one thinks that they have a bad sense of humor, talks too much, makes others uncomfortable, has a tendency to be boring, or is needy. But we all know people who are each of these things, and they're oblivious to it.

It's really hard to give harsh feedback to people along these lines, because these deficiencies feel so core to our being. They're actually not-- they can all be worked on and improved, but hearing them from a friend feels like a real blow. So we don't tell each other and we just deal with it.

Hard as it may be for either of us to believe, you and I probably both have weaknesses that grate on our friends, and we may never discover them.

Because of this, it's critical to be a better friend than you think you have to be. It's nice to say that we should all be the best friends we could possibly be, but there are real world constraints. You can only reach out to so many people per day. You can only do favors for so many people. You can only set up so many events. You only have so many hours in which you can listen to a friend's problems and try to work through them.

And so we compromise and we keep a fuzzy running tally. If I go to three cool events that a friend puts on, I know that I should really be doing something nice to reciprocate, and I'll shift my schedule to do that. Not because my friend requires it, but because it's the right thing to do and I want to be at least as good a friend to anyone as they are to me.

I'm likely pretty aware of every good thing I do for a friend, but I'm not aware of my hidden flaws that probably make me a slightly worse friend than I'd like to be. So I set the bar higher than it has to be and try to be a better friend than is necessary. At worst, I'm keeping pace and being a valuable friend, and at best I'm going over the top to be a really good friend. In either case, I avoid being a drag or someone who is maybe worth being friends with but comes with some baggage.

Maintaining Harmony

Harmony within groups of people is lack of friction. The more you can have everyone on the same page, the smoother things will go and the more time can be spent on high quality social activities. Friction comes in the form of bickering, indecision, pointless arguing, or personality clashes.

As a leader within your group, one of your responsibilities is to maintain harmony, even if you have to bear the cost of it. It's important to remember that you can bear responsibility for something even if it's not your own fault. You may not get overt credit for it, but your group will notice that things run better when you're around, and that goodwill will flow back to you.

Your primary tool in maintaining harmony is using awareness with social skills to see three steps ahead, identify pitfalls, and steer the conversation in a more positive direction.

Imagine that you're at a party, and three of your friends, Alice, Bob, and Charlie are talking. Alice and Bob are having a great time, but Charlie is getting bored and impatient. That's not a huge deal by itself, but you've noticed this happening a lot and you think that Charlie isn't feeling like he's a valued part of the group. You could go over and begin talking with him, asking him a lot of questions to communicate that he is a valued member of the group. Maybe you'd mention something he organized for the group last year and ask if he was thinking about doing it again this year.

Or imagine that two friends have been bickering the last few times you saw them, and now they're just avoiding each other. You're worried that they've given up trying to resolve things between themselves and are going to create a rift in the group. You might make a point of spending one-on-one time with each of them, asking what's going on, empathizing, and trying to come up with ideas to resolve the conflict.

Appreciating Your Friends

You know that feeling when you get a new phone? It's so shiny and small and fast. Everything looks great on it and it's a pleasure to use. You buy a case and a screen protector, and you're quite sure you'll never drop it or scuff it up. Never put it in the same pocket as your keys, like you did with your old phone. You look at your old phone and you can't stand to use it for another day.

We have an amazing capacity to become accustomed to what we have and to take it for granted. This happens with our personal possessions, but it also happens to less material things like the city we live in, and even our friends.

Your phone doesn't care how you treat it. Drop it, scratch it, scuff it up, and it will continue to work for you as best it can. That's not how relationships work, though. The more you appreciate and respect your friends, the better the relationship will work in general. John Gottman, a researcher at the University of Washington, studies couples to figure out what causes divorce. The biggest factor is contempt, which sounds a lot like the opposite of appreciation.

Appreciation isn't a passive process, a binary flag where you either appreciate your friends or you don't. It's an active process, one that calibrates your mind to subconsciously treat your friends really well.

Take a minute now and think about your friends.

Think about your friend group, your friends with whom you're slowly becoming even better friends, and even your old best friends with whom you don't talk anymore. Think about how they've impacted your life, how different things would be if you didn't have them. Think about the experiences shared, the conversations had, and the places you've been together.

Whenever you think things aren't running smoothly with your friends, when you're stressed out, or even when you're just waiting in line at the post office, repeat this exercise. If you really think about it, your friends are probably one of the most important factors in your life. That deserves some appreciation.

Putting it Together

Reading about strategies for improving social skills, making friends, and building friend groups, is an important and valuable thing to do. However, this is only half the battle at best. To actually reap the benefits from the seeds sowed in this book, you have to get out there and practice them.

Your first step should be to choose one or two important areas that you can practice with existing friends and family members, and focus on those. If nothing in particular jumped out at you, storytelling and becoming more aware of your social flaws would be a good starting point.

Strive for mastery on these fronts. There's no reason you can't become one of the top one percent of storytellers in the world. It's just a skill, and it's one that very few people actively practice. We all have our social deficiencies, but plenty of people have chiseled away at them to the point of having so few that they're not even noticeable.

As you work on these skills, remember what is at stake. Developing better social skills will strengthen your existing friendships and relationships with your family members, build new ones, allow you to get along better with strangers and acquaintances, and fill you with a confidence you may not have experienced before. The reward is high, so hard work can be easily justified.

Once you feel like you're almost always a net addition to groups that you join, and that your glaring social weaknesses have been eliminated, turn your focus to your social circle. Are there people with whom you regularly spend time whose presence isn't a positive one in your life? Maybe it's time to let them find friends better suited to them. Who are the people with whom you spend the most time, and how can you help build a cohesive friend group?

Although you can begin to make immediate improvements, the complete process of socially reinventing yourself and rebuilding your social skills could take a while, maybe years. Amongst people I know who have done this, though, the consensus is unanimous: the time spent is worth it, and is possibly the best investment of time you can make.

Made in the USA
Middletown, DE
31 January 2017